THE WORK OF ART

Stephen C. Pepper THE

WORK OF ART

Bloomington
INDIANA UNIVERSITY PRESS *1955*

N
70
.P37

DEDICATION

To my daughters, Elizabeth and Frances

PREFACE

THIS GROUP of essays is a sequel to the lectures I called "The Basis of Criticism in the Arts," given at Harvard in 1949. In the Harvard lectures the aim was to seek out the sources of the soundest critical criteria available for the arts. In the course of that search the object to which these criteria were to be applied inevitably also emerged for study. It is amazing how much can be said about an object without knowing what it is. Apparently, criticism in the arts has been doing that for a long time, and my own study of criticism managed to do the same quite unconcernedly, too, except for a twinge of conscience about the matter which issued in a supplementary essay, published with the Harvard lectures, which opened up the problem.

The analysis there was by no means satisfactory. But it did stimulate a good deal of discussion, and some of this got into print. So, when the invitation came to lecture on the Powell Foundation, nothing seemed so appropriate and timely for me as how then to cope with this problem of what precisely a work of art was and, particularly, what was the object of criticism. Actually, object and criteria are mutually dependent and hardly to be properly separated. So I hope that in this book the criteria discussed in the previous book will have found their proper object at last. At the same time, I felt the problem of the work of art was a sufficiently integral subject to stand on its own without requiring the background of the material of the previous study.

The book as it now appears is based on the Powell lectures, given at Indiana University in July, 1953, and on other lectures delivered at the University of California the following spring.

I want to thank the Philosophy Department of Indiana University for the honor of being invited to give the Powell Foundation lectures and Indiana University Press for stimulating me to expand the series for publication under their auspices.

STEPHEN C. PEPPER

Berkeley, California
April, 1955

CONTENTS

THE WORK OF ART

1

WHAT IS A WORK OF ART?

ONE OF the surprising things in the history of aesthetics is the small amount of attention given to the aesthetic object, or the work of art. Attention has been mainly directed upon aesthetic value or upon aesthetic experience. But the object that has that value or produces that experience has been largely neglected. Only within the last decade do we find some attempts at a description of its nature.

I should like in this chapter to press this inquiry perhaps a little further, or at least to see where we stand on the problem at the present time.

The first step in clarification of the problem is to realize that we are not dealing in this area with one object but with a little nest of related objects. It helps a lot just to become aware of this fact. For, if we think there must be only one object of aesthetic interest and that this is *the* work of art, we shall find ourselves blocked at the start by the competition of the several aesthetic objects each of which is making its own vigorous and legitimate claim to the title.

Let us have in mind, to begin with, one of the simplest of these nests of objects to describe, some picture of unquestioned aesthetic worth. Suppose we take the same picture Ushenko uses in his excellent analysis in his *Dynamics of Art* —Breughel's *Winter*. This is the sort of thing we generally refer to with innocent confidence as a work of art. Until the complexity of the problem has been brought to our attention, it probably does not occur to any of us that there is a problem here at all. We just point to the picture and indicate what we mean. We mean that what we point at is the work of art, Breughel's *Winter*.

But what are we pointing at? Perhaps we are pointing at the reproduction of the painting in Ushenko's book. Excellent as that reproduction is, we should probably agree that this is not the work of art itself, but merely a copy of it—a reproduction. The work of art itself is the picture Breughel himself painted, the one that can be found in the National Museum in Vienna. And yet we should not be too easily satisfied with this simple answer. There are many people—probably many among my readers—who have never seen the picture in Vienna. Nevertheless, they have, through the reproductions, some considerable acquaintance with the work of art. Many critics write learnedly and authoritatively about pictures and statues and buildings which they have never seen in the original. On first thought this seems ridiculous and rather hypocritical. But the situation is not so ridiculous on second thought. The reproduction is certainly a beautiful thing in itself. It is not as beautiful as the original, but all the very considerable beauty it has does come from the original. Breughel made that beauty, too—certainly not the photographer. All we ask of the photographer is technical fidelity. Fidelity to what? To Breughel's picture, of course. Breughel's original—the aesthetic object of aesthetic worth—is somehow transmitted through the reproduction. Something is lost in the transmission, like seeing the original from the length of the gallery instead of nearby in the most favorable position. But if the beauty of the reproduction is not the beauty of the original, who was the genius who created the beauty of the reproduction? Of course, it was Breughel himself. So in pointing

at the reproduction as the work of art called
Breughel's *Winter,* you and I are not being as
ridiculous as we first thought.

When we consider pictures which are prints
—such as etchings, lithographs, woodblocks—
then, literally, each print is an original copy of
the work of art. And so with the casts of bronzes.
And so with every copy of a book in literature,
and every performance in music and drama.

So what are we pointing at when we point at
a work of art?

The problem begins to unfold. Let me distinguish three objects in this nest of objects. There
is first what may be called the vehicle—that
continuously existing object, generally physical
in nature, which carries the aesthetic values,
preserves them and controls them for perception. For Breughel's *Winter*—and now for
a while we shall imagine we are before his
original—the vehicle for this picture is the canvas covered with various oil pigments in the
Vienna museum. As a physical object this picture, this vehicle, can be carried about, loaned
to other museums, stored in a salt mine, sold as
merchandise, cleaned, damaged, restored, etc.
If carefully described, it would probably be de-

scribed in physical and chemical terms. Few writers would consider the vehicle as literally an object of aesthetic worth. It is an instrument for the production, preservation, and control of the object of aesthetic worth.

Then, secondly, I wish to distinguish the object of immediate perception. This is the experience a spectator has at any one time when stimulated by the vehicle. This is the object we see and feel and fill with meaning. It has a date and a location. Many will set the location within our bodies. Definitely our bodies are much involved in the object of immediacy. Our sense organs, our eyes in this instance, give us the colors and the lines and the shape; and our brains presumably give us the meanings of the represented objects dependent on learning and memory; and our endocrine systems presumably contribute to our emotions. Our bodies are extensively involved in the perceptual response. Whether the content of the perception is limited to the activities of our bodies, or only centered there, in either circumstance the locus of the object of immediacy is in the region of our bodily responses. And the duration of an object of immediacy is a certain spread of time, but actually no longer than the so-called specious present, the time that can be taken in intuitively at a single act of attention.

The object of immediacy is only a few seconds long, then. This brings out the fact that the aesthetic perception of a poem or a piece of music requires a series of perceptive immediacies. For the beginning of a melody has passed out of the span of immediacy before the end of it comes. We get the contour of the whole melody when it is completed, but not through the direct stimulation of its sounds from end to end of a single attention span. A single motive of the melody may be intuited that way, like a phrase of a sentence, but not the whole melody or the whole sentence, for the attention span is limited to a few seconds.

The need of a succession of perceptive immediacies to obtain one integral perception of a poem or a melody is here obvious enough. A bit of reflection will show that the same is true of a spatial work of art like a picture or a statue. A statue in the round clearly demands that the spectator see all sides of it for a single integral perception of the whole statue. A series of perceptive immediacies is required for a single complete perception of the statue just as for the poem or melody. Less obviously, but just as surely, a series of such immediacies is required for an integral perception of a picture like Breughel's *Winter*. At the first glance we perhaps see the men and the dogs, or the parallel verticals of the trees cutting a long diagonal. Then we are drawn to notice other details of the picture, and it requires some minutes to grasp and respond to even the main elements of composition and representation embedded in the picture.

So, just in a single perception of a work of art, we run into some unexpected complexities. What is usually called a single perception—say the first time one hears a musical composition or sees a picture—is already not one act of perceptual response but a succession of such acts. Yet somehow we obtain something of an integral perception of the work and of the series of perceptive immediacies.

Before we go any further let us be quite clear with ourselves concerning the object of immediacy. It is very often assumed in aesthetic discussions that this is the pivotal aesthetic object and that this is an object of direct sensory stimulation. Many who speak of an "aesthetic surface" appear to have these assumptions implicit. There is the suggestion that a pure aesthetic experience is a purely receptive one, discriminating the sensuous effects and the formal relations impressed upon a spectator by the stimulus object. The derivation of "aesthetic" from the Greek "aesthesis," meaning "sensuous," is often appealed to. Meanings, references, and synthetic activities of the mind are admitted into the aesthetic experience grudgingly. Even representation is questionably aesthetic, and social references even more so. The attraction to this view is mainly, I feel, its supposed intuitive ultimacy in the object of immediacy.

The object of sensuous immediacy is, of course, necessary and pivotal as the source of all aesthetic data, but it is not sufficient. It is not sufficient, as we have just seen, for even one integral perception of a work of art. A whole melody of usual length cannot possibly be a perceptual object of direct stimulation, because the initial sound stimuli are way out of the attention span when the terminal stimuli of the melody are being responded to. The earlier phrases of a melody have to be referred to or reached by some process of memory while the last phrase is being played, in order that the melody as a whole may be intuited. Even in the aesthetic perception of a single simple melody there must be a synthetic incorporation of past meanings into a present content. A term for this process, become current through Dewey's prestige, is "funding." Funding is the fusion of meanings from past experiences into a present experience. The earlier perceptions of a melody are thus funded into the later ones, and thence arises our capacity for getting the integral sense of a melody from a series of short-span perceptual immediacies.

The necessity of funding even for rather simple aesthetic perceptions shows up at once the inadequacy of any theory that tries to limit the aesthetic field to that of pure sensuous immediacy. There is practically no work of art—perhaps none—that does not require some funding for its perception. The least that could be suggested is that the funding should be limited to the memories of earlier sensuous responses. But if sensuous funding is permissible, why not any other sorts of meaning so long as they can be relevantly embodied into an aesthetic perception?

This rather new concept of funding deserves some closer examination. It includes another concept, also rather new in aesthetic descriptions, the concept of fusion. As just pointed out, funding is fusion of memory elements into a present perception. We call memories funding when they give a tone or atmosphere to the content of direct sensuous stimulation. It is not funding if no memory elements are present in a perception. It is not funding if the memory is separately distinguishable from the direct sensuous material. Funding is something between the two. It is the fusion of memory with sensuous immediacy so as to give the effect of an enriched immediacy.

This effect was often noticed by writers describing the aesthetic perception even before Dewey pinpointed it with a name. In his chapter on "Expression" in *The Sense of Beauty,* Santayana describes the effect with sensitive appreciation and makes it definitive of aesthetic expression. And, as you will see, he does not limit funding to sensuous memories only but includes all meaning. He says: "We not only construct visible unities and recognizable types, but remain aware of their affinities to what is not at the time perceived; that is, we find in them a certain tendency and quality, not original to them, a meaning and a tone, which upon investigation we shall see to have been the proper characteristics of other objects and feelings, associated with them once in our experience. The hushed reverberations of these associated feelings continue in the brain, and by modifying our present reaction, colour the image upon which our attention is fixed. The quality thus acquired by objects through association is what we call their expression."

And again, emphasizing the difference between discursive association and aesthetic expression, he says, "Thus the mementos of a lost friend do not become beautiful by virtue of the sentimental associations which may make them precious. The value is confined to the images of the memory; they are too clear to let any of that value escape and diffuse itself over the rest of our consciousness, and beautify the objects which we actually behold. We say explicitly: I value this trifle for its associations. And so long as this division continues, the worth of the thing is not for us aesthetic.

"But a little dimming of our memory will often make it so. Let the images of the past fade, let them remain simply as a halo and suggestion of happiness hanging about a scene; then this scene . . . will have a deep and intimate charm; . . . The treasures of the memory have been melted and dissolved, and are now gilding the object that supplants them; they are giving this object expression."

And again, ". . . I may receive a letter full of the most joyous news, but neither the paper, nor the writing, nor the style, need seem beautiful to me. Not until I confound the impressions, and suffuse the symbols themselves with the emotions they arouse, and find joy and sweetness in the very words I hear, will the expressiveness constitute a beauty; as when they sing, *Gloria in excelsis Deo*." [1]

"Melt," "dissolve," "confound," "suffuse," Santayana spreads out the synonyms of fusion all but naming the word which Dewey has practically rendered technical. He is saying that only when memory fuses in this way have we aesthetic expression. I am not concerned here with Santayana's limitation of aesthetic associations to those that are fused. I would not wish always to insist upon this requirement. But I am anxious that we should note what he is referring to, and that we should see that we are all familiar with the effect, even though perhaps we may not have noticed its great aesthetic importance.

There is a famous passage of Bosanquet's in his *Three Lectures on Aesthetic* which makes the same point. Here is a man of a totally different school of philosophy from Santayana, as both are different from Dewey, and he also sees the effect of funding and notes its aesthetic importance. I will briefly quote this passage and then move on to the bearing of this effect on our problem: ". . . the appearance which is the object will . . . fail to be a satisfactory embodiment of feeling, unless it is at least satisfactory as a mere pattern, . . . but also and additionally, in harmony with this satisfactoriness, it must be satisfactorily expressive through the concrete character of that which it reppresents. You must interpret the Discobolos through your experience of human bodies; and I suppose that your sense of the life in the abstract pattern is itself actually amplified and intensified by this deeper experience. . . . the expressiveness of the abstract pattern penetrates, by experience used in the service of the imagination, into the realm of nature and man, and extends itself over and appropriates ground that is primarily representative and gains at the same time a deeper significance from it. . . . It should be noted that we exclude mere association from the expressive connection which we demand. The expressiveness must be in some degree inherent in the form. . . . Mere association brings us down at once to the level of knowledge of fact, as when my old portmanteau reminds me of Florence." [2]

Now if we see what fusion of memories is within a present perception, we can show how it operates within the radius of a work of art. Santayana and Bosanquet were intent on exhibiting the fact of funding and its power to bring associative materials from past experience into a fused present perception. They were intent upon gathering up the relevant material for an aesthetic perception. Our interest in funding and fusion at the present juncture is a little different. It is to show how a present perception can enfold and have telescoped into it a great quantity of previous perceptions of the *same* object. We are interested in a certain cumulative effect of fusion towards the comprehension of a single stimulating object—towards a total funded perception of a single work of art.

Our problem is how it may be possible to obtain an adequate perception of a complex object like a work of art and on what grounds we may call one perception more adequate than another. The concept of funding goes a long way towards solving that problem.

The perception of a complex object like Breughel's *Winter* is necessarily selective and partial. No one in a single act of perception can experience the totality of that picture in all its discriminated detail. But through funding one can approach that ideal. The first perception of a work of art by an experienced spectator is necessarily very thin and inadequate. We can easily get the sense of this meagreness by looking at, or listening to, some most recent production of a school of art in some medium with which we are still unfamiliar. A few details catch our attention. For the rest we are often much confused and suspect that we are pretty blind. Here the growing adequacy of successive perceptions with increasing discrimination is obvious enough. But even for the experienced beholder, it takes time and a multiplicity of perceptions to discriminate the relevant details. Now, as we said earlier, one pays attention to the large compositional effect; then to details of pattern, to contrasts, repetitions, echoes of themes; then to the space representation, the pattern on the picture plane, and the pattern in depth; then to the figures represented; then to the activities of the figures and their interrelationships—and so on. Familiar as one may be with Breughel's *Winter* and absorbed as one may be in its relevant traits, one's perceptions are still selective and concentrate now on certain features to delight in, now on others. How, then, ever to get the perceptions of the whole picture?

It is through funding that a person does it. When one is focusing his attention on the figures in the foreground, he is aware of the figures and hills in the background in the fringe of his vision and the memory of an attentive focusing upon them is funded into the perception of the figures in the foreground. So all the past perceptions of the picture are added to the present perception in the way of "hushed reverberations." Literally one can never see the whole picture in all its detail in focus at one time. But one can feel the whole picture in all its detail in a funded consciousness with certain details in clear focus and the rest fused into these as memories of their character and interrelationships.

When we come into a strange town, we can see only what is directly before our eyes. What happens up each street, and how the streets turn, and where the parks are and the river and the bridges, and where the stores are and the city hall and the residential area are all hidden to us. But when we have been in the town awhile, the perception of each street contains a feeling of its relations with every other street, and the tone of a street a block away from the freight yards has the clatter of the freight cars in it already, and the contrasting peace of the park beyond by the river and the swimming pool are right there in the very block we are moving along.

So it is in a work of art, in Breughel's picture. With familiarity we get to feel every detail funded into any detail we may be looking at. There is only this difference between the town and the picture, that we think of the town as an object primarily in terms of its practical physical relationships rather than in terms of its total perceivable character, whereas we think of the work of art and evaluate it primarily in terms of its total perceivable character rather than in terms of its physical vehicle.

Through funding—for this is the significant point we are stressing—the total character of a work of art is describably perceivable. This total character is definable and open to verification. Through funding previous perceptions of details here, here, and here in the work of art can be interrelated and through memory fused into the subsequent perception of other details. Thus a progression of cumulative funding of perceptions can be described, leading to the ideal of a set of totally funded perceptions of the work. The object of aesthetic criticism is this ideal set of fully funded perceptions of all the relevant details stimulated by the physical vehicle of the work of art.

But I am getting a little ahead of my sequence. I showed the need of considering the thing we call a work of art as a nest of objects. I am in fact suggesting that it consists of three closely interrelated objects: First, the physical vehicle; second, the object of perceptual immediacy. These two objects within the nest of the total work of art we have so far been describing. The third which we now come to I shall call the object of criticism.

The physical vehicle is the continuous enduring control object which is the source of stimulation for the succession of fugitive objects of perceptual immediacy. The object of criticism is some sort of synthesis or evaluative goal of the sequence of perceptual immediacies. The first object, the vehicle, is as enduring as the physical and cultural materials of which it is composed. The third object, the object of criticism, is equally enduring because it is in the nature of a potentiality or dispositional property of the vehicle. It is the full potentiality of aesthetic perception available to the aesthetic vehicle. But what connects the two and actualizes both for aesthetic appreciation is the sequence of perceptual immediacies stimulated by the vehicle. The second object is the actual object of immediate aesthetic experience. This object, however, is fugitive. It lasts but a few moments and is gone. There may be a continuous succession of immediate perceptions, as in listening to a symphony or contemplating a painting for a long time. But the length of a single stretch of immediacy cannot exceed a specious present.

It is this fact that gives an illusory support to the view that there are as many works of art as there are perceptions of it, and that one perception is as good as another, and that there is no verifiable significance in saying that one perception is less adequate aesthetically than another. One part of the answer to this view is the evidence for the operation of funding. That is why I have spent some time on this concept.

The sequence of perceptions stimulated by the vehicle of a work of art are not all on a level. They are, according to the very thesis of the relativistic view itself, not all the same. They are, in fact, for any one observer nearly all different.

But the differences are not random, as the relativistic view tends to let one think. The differences are, on the whole, ordered in a certain direction. The sequence of perceptions represents a cumulative funding of the discriminations of the earlier perceptions into the later. The later perceptions are on the whole more adequate responses to the total stimulating capacity of the physical vehicle than the earlier ones. We ordinarily call them more discriminating. This result is largely due to funding. This could suggest at once the idea that the object of criticism is the last most fully funded perception in a series of perceptual immediacies. This conception of the third of our three objects comprising the nest of objects we call the work of art is getting warm but is not quite all that is needed.

What is left out is something that has already been alluded to in passing several times. It is the concept of relevancy. It is this concept along with funding, and even more than funding, that determines the third of our nest of objects that make up the work of art, the object of criticism.

For it must now be evident that the object of immediacy, unless further qualified, is not exactly what is prized and praised as the great

Breughel masterpiece, as one of the very great aesthetic works of western culture. Hundreds of people pass before the canvas, getting some sort of perception of it—some sort of object of immediacy. Most of these perceptions we should consider far short of an adequate perception of the picture. They do not any one of them, even when highly funded, present Breughel's great painting. They are, to be sure, the objects which embody the spectators' responses, the objects liked or disliked or otherwise evaluated by the several spectators. But where among these is Breughel's great painting? What is the object to which the evaluative term "great" is ascribed?

It would be strange if the object of criticism were not in some sense a perceptual object. But how can it be a perceptual object, when the spectators exhibit such variability in their perceptual responses?

An outside possibility, as I have said, is that there is no such object—the position, namely, of the aesthetic relativist. For this man, there is the vehicle or control object. And there are a variety of responses to that object yielding objects of perception. These may be evaluated in a variety of ways—for their enjoyment, their utility, or what not. But there is no sense, says he,

in saying that there is an object of criticism
over and above these perceptions. If one is suggested, he says, it would be just somebody else's
perception, or a fiction.

Nevertheless, there is a persistent notion that
somewhere in this context there is an object de-
serving the attribute of greatness, which can be
described and which people can be expected to
respect—an object that has an objective claim.
Can this notion be substantiated? Or is it just a
bit of wishful thinking? I believe it can be substantiated. But the description I offer must not
be regarded as more than an approximation of
the truth of the matter.

You will notice that we do not ascribe "greatness" to a momentary perception. I may speak
of my present perception of Breughel's *Winter*
as "satisfactory," or "exhilarating," but not as
"great." I speak of having a satisfying perception of Breughel's great masterpiece. The masterpiece is something different from a perception
of it.

You will notice also that we do not speak of
a piece of canvas with pigment patches on it
as "great." We speak of the canvas as being in
good condition, or in need of a cleaning, or as

having been tampered with and touched up by renovators. But not except as a figure of speech, in the way we call a ship a sail, would we call a masterpiece a canvas, even with the addition of the pigments. A canvas is involved in a masterpiece. It is the vehicle for it. But it is not literally the "great" aesthetic object.

So, the object we call "great" cannot be identified with any one momentary perception, nor with the vehicle that stimulates perceptions. Nor is it probable, considering the amount of cultural material devoted to the study and description and evaluation of great works of art, that no such objects exist. Histories of art and music and literature, libraries of art criticism and aesthetics, are not likely to be about nothing.

If we examine the content of the studies about works of art, we will see that the issues raised are all about matters of perceptual content. They are not, however, issues over what one spectator may have perceived. The spectator's report of his perception is generally accepted at face value. The issues arise over whether the spectator should not have perceived something more or something different. There is also a lot about the cultivation of taste, the sharpening of one's discriminations, and the broadening of one's interests for appreciative perception of a great work of art.

The control object for all these discussions is, of course, the vehicle, and the content is perceptions stimulated in spectators by the vehicle—not one perception but a collection and a selection of them. The object of criticism is some sort of assemblage of perceptions. The problem is to describe the nature and the control of this assemblage.

It might be said as a first guess that the object of criticism is the totality of all perceptions stimulated by the vehicle. But this idea neglects the evidence of progressive selection among these perceptions. It neglects the facts of funding and of aesthetic relevancy.

Perceptual material relative to an aesthetic vehicle is selected for relevancy on two main grounds. The one is that the vehicle contains the direct stimulus of a sensory quality for normal response. The other is that the associative anticipations aroused by the sensory material are so organized as to confirm the anticipations over and over again. The one is the stimulus test, the other the internal reference test. Both are subject to verification. The colors and lines and shapes to be found in the Breughel are relevant, in part at least, to the stimulus test; the representation of men, animals, trees, snow and ice and the suggestions of cold, of distance, of village life, and of social activities are relevant by the internal reference test. A description of a work of art is a description of these relevant perceptual details. And a large part of the discussion to be found in books of art and aesthetics is over matters of relevancy. For it is by means of the tests of relevancy that one determines what is or is not in the work of art for appreciation.

With this explanation, we may now describe the object of criticism as the totality of relevant material based on the perceptions stimulated by an aesthetic vehicle.

Relevancy, it may be noticed, however, makes demands upon the spectator as well as upon the vehicle. The spectator must have normal sense organs to respond to the stimuli of the vehicle. Moreover, he is expected to have acute discriminations if these are called for. Often such discrimination requires experience and learning, as, for instance, an awareness of precise pitch differences within a musical scale, and of chords, and of the tensions of tonality. Thus sense discrimination shades over into cultural references and the two are sometimes hard to separate. A cultivated ear and eye is often demanded for the very understanding of a work of art. The cultivation may be mainly in sensory discrimination, but it may be also a cultural conditioning for the appreciation of a whole style of art, to say nothing of significant cultural references that may appear in the work. There is also an emotional cultivation that may be called for and a number of other demands upon the spectator which aesthetic books enlarge upon. In short, relevancy also demands a competent spectator.

This reflection makes possible another description of the object of criticism. It is the object perceived by a person who has become a competent spectator. But notice it is not the taste of the competent spectator that defines the object but his capacity to respond to the relevant perceptions. The pivot of the question is the relevant materials. The object of criticism, what we call the "great" work of art, is the collection and organization of these relevant materials stimulated by the vehicle.

A few conclusions can now be drawn.

First, our description above shows that an object of criticism distinct from the vehicle or the momentary perception of a work of art can be indicated.

Second, this object is verifiable by the tests of relevancy and of competence in the responses of a spectator. It is accordingly cognitively objective.

Third, the object is theoretically capable of being immediately experienced, possibly not in one single perception, but in a series of perceptions all the content of which is relevant. This is made possible by the process of funding, through which earlier perceptions fuse their contents with later ones making possible an intuitive sense of a perceptual whole spreading over a wide period of discrete stimulation.

Fourth, for the most part, however, and necessarily so in very complex works, the object of criticism is an objectively defined ideal rather than a particular funded perception. It may be thus regarded as a dispositional property of the vehicle. The stimulus pattern of the vehicle has the capacity of generating the funded system of relevant perceptions which constitutes the object of criticism.

Fifth, most persons' perceptions of a work of art are, accordingly, various degrees of approximation to the complete potential object of criticism. Insofar as they fall short, they are properly to be regarded as false or inadequate, just as a perception of a practical object is false if it distorts or overlooks some of the stimulus conditions. As a man looking at a leaf may fail to perceive its details and structure, seeing only an oval green patch with some meaningless humpy lines crossing it, so a man listening to a symphony or looking at Breughel's *Winter* may fail to perceive most of it. Neither of these perceptions would be true to their object—the one botanically, the other aesthetically. And the consequence of failing to perceive the aesthetic object is that it cannot be appreciated—if indeed any separation is possible between the appreciation of a great work of art and its fully funded relevant perception.

2

CAN A JUDGMENT OF BEAUTY
BE TRUE?

THERE IS a strange doctrine making the rounds just now to the effect that value judgments cannot be true. The reason put forward is not the modest one that we have not sufficient data to establish their truth and so must be content with probability somewhat short of the truth. The reason is a definitional one, that a value judgment by fiat is an emotional expression and so removed from the area of cognitive statements which may be true or false.

The reasoning that leads up to this conclusion goes like this: A value judgment is an expression containing such words as "good," "bad," "right," "wrong," "beautiful," "ugly," "ought," "ought not," and the like. Then it is stated that an expression, "X is good," is entirely different in its meaning from an expression such as "X is white." "X is white" is a true or false cognitive

41

statement; on the other hand, "X is good," even though it is grammatically similar to "X is white," is a concealed command or wish stated in declarative form. "X is white" is a declarative sentence asserting that some object has the character "whiteness." The object may in truth have or not have this character and so the sentence can be verified. But the sentence "X is good" is not a declarative sentence but a command or wish. It is an imperative or an optative. It does not assert that some object has a character "goodness." It is a command or a wish that someone should take a certain attitude towards X. Commands and wishes are neither true nor false. If I say, "Open the window," I have not said anything true or false. To utter the expression, "An open window is good," is, in the value-judgment theory, to say the same thing in a gentler but more ambiguous way. In neither instance have I made any assertion about the window or about any other fact in the world. I have simply expressed my attitude. I have simply made a vocal gesture as devoid of truth as if I pounded my fist on the table, or gave a man a push.

There is usually, perhaps always, according to the value-judgment theory, a little appendix of meaning added to a value-judgment expression which a cry of pain or kick in the shins does not possess; namely, that the person addressed should accept the same attitude. Particularly if the command is expressed in the form "the window *ought* to be open," this appendix of a public appeal becomes prominent. But it is quickly added by the emotivists, i.e., the exponents of the present theory, that this appeal is only a persuasive one and has nothing to do with true or false propositions that can be asserted about the window or with the situation in which the window is placed.

This emotive theory clearly has a direct bearing on our discussion in the previous chapter regarding the work of art. For our conclusion then was that the object of criticism is an empirically describable object open to cognitive verification. Within the compass of what is roughly called "the work of art," we found three interrelated objects, it will be recalled: First, there was the vehicle or control object such as the canvas for a picture, the printed page for a poem; second, there was the immediate fugitive perception stimulated by the vehicle; and, third, there was the object of criticism which is a dispositional property of the vehicle and refers to the funded perception or system of perceptions of a fully competent observer stimulated by the vehicle.

According to our analysis, a description of any one of these three objects would be in the nature of a declarative sentence, true or false. Likewise, a description of any discrepancies between the character of some person's reported perception of the vehicle and the character of the final funded system of relevant perceptions constituting the object of criticism, so far as ascertained, would be in the nature of a declarative sentence, true or false.

It follows in our view that there is at least one acceptable significance of the expression of "ought" which is declarative in form and may be true or false. This is an assertion to the effect that for a full appreciation of a work of art a man's immediate perceptions ought to approximate as closely as possible the character of the fully funded relevant perceptions constituting the object of criticism.

What is indicated in this view is something implicitly denied by the value-judgment theorists, namely, that under the guidance of the vehicle as a control object there is a factually describable process of progressive discrimination and appreciation of the object of criticism, which is the goal of this process. The dynamics for the process lies in the impulses which attract the spectator to respond to the object in the beginning. Continued attraction to the object leads to continued response for the maximum value to be found in it, and this cumulative process tends to continue until all the relevant content is attained which, when attained, constitutes the object of criticism itself—the terminus and implicit goal of the whole process.

Such a process is what I should like to call a "selective system." The characteristic of a selective system is that a single dynamic element directs action at two levels at once, a long-range level, such as a goal, and a short-range level, such as a tentative attempt to attain the goal. The attempt has to be made if the goal is to be reached at all, and the motivation for the attempt is the very motivation that directs the organism to the goal. But if the goal is not known ahead, or if skills and causal relationships have to be learned to reach the goal, then the attempts on the way to the goal are necessarily liable to error. The error is a factual occurrence and can be truly described, and the fact that it *ought* not to have occurred (which is the common way of calling attention to it) can also be truly described by comparing it with the act that would have led to the goal and *ought* to have been performed. Through the dynamics of a selective system, the act that ought to be performed presently will be performed, since the dynamics of the system sees to it that the organism is continuously attracted towards the goal. The charge upon the goal is the factual sanction—the verifiable sanction—for the goal as a value criterion. A selective system is a factual process that operates on two levels and selects acts which it initiates and which it tries out on a subordinate level, testing how far they contribute towards the attainment of an act aimed for on a superordinate level.

An appetitive purposive structure such as the pursuit of food by a hungry animal, or the pursuit of knowledge by an inquisitive one, is a prime example of a selective system.

The dynamic process of the appreciation of a work of art is another such selective system. It has peculiarities of its own, however, which distinguish it from the working of an everyday practical purpose. The difference can be best summarized by saying that the dynamics of appreciation is consummatory, whereas that of a practical purpose is anticipatory. In developing the contrast between the two, many qualifications would need to be made. But at present it is more important to see that the appreciation of a work of art is a progressive selective process and to see how, in general, it differs from the process of a practical purpose, than to be minutely precise in the differentiation of the two.

A practical purpose, as we generally encounter it, is anticipatory. We have knowledge or foresight of the goal which we set before us as an end through the dynamics of some drive, and we proceed to seek out means for attaining the goal. We may not know the means and we may make errors along the way in our selection of means. Our acts in selecting the means are good or bad in proportion as these acts are, on the one hand, conducive to the attainment of the goal, or, on the other hand, mistaken and delaying. We speak of a mistaken act as an error and as one we *ought not* to have performed. The true instrumental act when discovered is the one, we say, we *ought* all along to have performed. Through the selective system of an appetitive purpose at least one sense of "ought" thus obtains a factual or declarative description.

How does it get this description? It gets it

by the fact that a single dynamic agent, a purposive drive in this instance, is acting on two
levels at the same time. It is driving the organism on a superordinate or upper level towards
a goal, and in pursuance of this process it is also
driving the organism on a subordinate or lower
level towards a means. The very drive that impels the organism to the goal impels it to the
means as an essential part of the same complex
activity. A highly structured act is here unfold-
ing through time. It is a *Gestalt*-like process. It
is not a mere succession of bead-like acts, as
though the terminal goal-seeking act only followed upon a means-seeking act, as though the
goal-seeking act did not begin until after the
means-seeking act was over. The goal-seeking
act is going on at the same time as the means-
seeking act, and these two acts are upper and
lower levels of the same structure and both are
impelled, motivated, by the same drive. The
drive that gives its emotional value to the goal
gives its value simultaneously to the means, and
the value of the goal is the norm; for, if the
means fails to lead to the goal, the drive at once
ceases to charge the means. The emotional value
of the means is, in fact, relative to that of the
end. That is the way this dynamic structure ac-

tually operates. By the very nature of a purposive structure the anticipatory thought of the goal charged by a drive selects pro or con a means charged by that same drive. Therefore, the means is good if it has the properties conducive to the attainment of the goal, bad if it doesn't. To state that the means is good is, thus, in a declarative sentence (true or false) to ascribe relational properties to that object just as much as to state that the object is heavy or above some other object in space. It is to attribute to the object the property of being wanted as a means and so of having causal relations leading to another object wanted as an end. All of this is factual, open to description, true or false.

I hope the reader will forgive me this expansion upon the obvious. But I must make it because I wish to point out for you clearly the analogous situation which holds in the process of a spectator's coming into the full appreciation of a work of art. The two processes have certain differences, but they are alike in this, which is crucial for the present issue regarding the declarative nature of judgments of beauty: namely, that both are selective systems and, as such, institute norms and selections of acts pro and con under those norms and by the very dynamics that institutes the norms. The process of a spectator's appreciation of a work of art is also a two-level selective process by which tentative acts are selected pro and con with reference to a potential terminus of the process set up by the dynamics of the process itself.

Let me take a very simple illustration. Think of yourself entering a gallery of an art museum. Suppose your eye catches a picture at the end of the room which attracts your attention and arouses your incipient admiration. Do you stop at the doorway and there relish the experience? No, pleasant as the picture is at that distance, it would be tantalizing to be kept there at a distance. The very consummatory structure of the situation draws you into the room to a position neither too near nor too far, where the colors and shapes are to be seen at their best. If there is a glass over the picture, you will move so that all glare is eliminated. In short, in a consummatory field of activity a person is drawn to the optimum condition of consummatory response with respect to the object—and, when the object is a work of art, specifically with respect to the stimulating aesthetic vehicle. And all positions or conditions less than the optimum are by the dynamics of the field rejected as less good than the optimum to which the dynamics of the field draws the spectator.

And similarly with music. We seek a location neither too near nor too far, where the sounds come at a consummatory optimum. To hear good music in the distance is to be drawn towards it where it can be heard best. The Pied Piper in the fable drew the children after him by means of this principle. They followed him because to stay behind as he moved forward was to drop out of the area of optimum reception. And our manipulation of the volume and the tone of a phonograph has the same significance.

We may call this the consummatory principle. It is the tendency to make the most of the consummatory field. The dynamics of the field draws the agent to the optimum area of satisfaction.

Now, if we have grasped the principle, we see that it is a selective system like an appetitive drive. In fact, it is the terminal phase of a positive desire. For the structure of a purposive act motivated by an appetitive drive like hunger is such as to draw an organism as quickly as possible to the consummatory field where the drive can attain quiescence. Acts are selected as right or wrong in proportion as they conduce or fail to conduce to the attainment of the consummatory field. But, having attained that field, then (barring the pressure of a practical emergency) the principle of action changes to that of maximizing satisfaction in the field. Acts are selected as right or wrong in proportion as they increase or decrease the available satisfaction, in proportion as they approach to or recede from areas of optimum reception. That the principle of selection changes within the consummatory field from what it was in the approach to this field can be seen by the fact that outside the field the quicker the activity is over the better, whereas within the field the longer the period of activity the better. The trend for the optimum of stimulation within the field has the effect of holding the organism there as long as possible. This is, of course, just a more detailed description of the well-recognized contrast between practical achievement and aesthetic contemplation. For practical achievement, the rule of the shortest path holds—the speedier the better. But for aesthetic enjoyment, the longer the better.

The point for us to note, however, is that the consummatory principle, which seeks to intensify and draw out enjoyment, is a selective principle. This point is often missed. Even in the

very simple examples we have just offered the
selective operation of the consummatory field
emerges. The structure of the field causes a person who moves from a more to a less favorable
position within the field to consider his movement an error and to correct it to a better position. And so from better to better positions the
person moves until he finds the optimum position which actually has been operating all the
time as the norm for the correctness and incorrectness of every move of the spectator within
the field. It is a natural norm determined by the
structure of the specific consummatory field and
is describable in declarative sentences just as a
physicist might describe a magnetic field.

The dynamics of this selective system, like
that of a purposive structure relating means and
end, is such that the impulse for the optimum is
the same as that which motivates the error in
the approach to the optimum. Just as the drive
which charges the anticipation of the end is the
very one that charges the incorrect choice of a
means so that in the very dynamics of the system
the means acknowledges its incorrectness by
virtue of the end; so here the consummatory
principle by which the organism seeks to maximize its enjoyment in the consummatory field

determines both the optimum point and the points of lesser receptivity. In this way a movement into a less favorable position is acknowledged as an error by the same dynamics that leads the organism to correct its error and feel its way towards the optimum.

Let us note, too, that the point of optimum receptivity is not known to the organism ahead of his responses in the consummatory field, unless he has had previous experience and remembers. Where is the best point to see a picture, or to listen to a piano? One has to move around in the consummatory area and find out. Nevertheless, that point is settled by the very structure of the field. It is a dispositional property of the situation. For the organism moving about in the field it is the ideal and norm of correctness of all his actions in the field. It is the place where he *ought* to be. And this is a declarative statement concerning the structure of the field!

Now, I think you can see where all these preliminaries are heading. They point to the statement that the object of criticism is the terminal area of optimum receptivity for the vehicle of a work of art.

For consider what is sought in the fullness of contemplation of a picture like Breughel's

Winter. To stand before it in the most favorable position under a favorable light is a beginning. But to perceive all the relevant details and to gather them up in successive discriminations and fundings of the content of the picture are parts of the same process. The balance and tensions of the forms, the linear design, the drama of the represented scene, and the attendant emotions are all in the consummatory field of the picture as truly as the point of most favorable visibility. The discriminative mind is drawn to find these in the consummatory field of this picture as compellingly as the body is attracted from the door at the end of the gallery to the optimum position a few feet in front of the picture. The search for this optimum consummatory area will be tentative and accompanied by many incorrect responses, just as a naive perceiver's search for the optimum position of visibility would be. The incorrect responses are the mistaking of irrelevant for relevant details in the object of criticism.

If I have made my point, there is no need to argue further about the basic issue of this discussion. For if the object of criticism is the optimum area of appreciation of the relevant characters stimulated by the vehicle of a work of art, then this is a matter of description and any description a writer gives of it will be true or false. If a writer describes his response to a work as though this were authoritative and yet leaves out many relevant features or inserts some irrelevant ones, he is making a false judgment which the consummatory field of the work will itself in time correct through the later discriminations of this same man, or of some other man more discriminating than he. If some spectator fails to reach the optimum point of visibility for a picture, the point is still there in the consummatory field, drawing any interested person to reach it who enters the field and stays there long enough. So also with the object of criticism as the optimum area of aesthetic contemplation.

For the point I am making is that an aesthetic judgment about a work of art, in at least one significant and common sense of the term, is a judgment about the capacity of the work for giving satisfaction to a discriminating perceiver, and that this is a judgment which is at once true or false and evaluative. When a critic says Breughel's *Winter* is "good" he is affirming a high degree of satisfaction to be obtained in the optimum perception of the work. He is not requesting anyone to agree with him, though he does expect other men as discriminating as he himself to confirm the truth of his judgment. The reason for this expectation is that the judgment refers to the norm of a selective system— namely, that system which operates in the consummatory field for the maximizing of satisfaction under the control of an enduring vehicle. For it is, of course, the facts of the situation that justify the prediction. For when a person is attracted to an object in the consummatory field, he does tend to adjust his behavior in the direction of the optimum response in respect to the controlling vehicle. In this operation of the selective system, the errors are predicted along with the successive approaches to complete appreciation.

When a critic states that Breughel's *Winter* is beautiful, he is accordingly referring to a consummatory field and the operation of a selective system within that field. He is referring to an area of optimum receptivity and to the content of response obtainable in that area. He may describe this content of the relevant characters of the fully appreciated picture in great detail. These characters will include emotions and feelings as well as colors, lines, and representational meanings. He is asserting in declarative terms that this is the response a person will get if he maximizes the relevant satisfactions in this consummatory area. His statement is of the "if-then" form and recognizes that most persons entering this consummatory field will have many inadequate perceptions of the picture on their way towards an optimum response. The ordinary way of expressing the discrepancy between the inadequate perceptions and the optimum response is that these perceptions are not what they ought to be, for they ought to be the perception of the optimum response. In making this normative statement the critic is not commanding other people to make their perceptions conform to his. On the contrary, he is showing these people the ultimate perception they themselves are trying to attain by their entrance into the consummatory field and by their attraction to this object. The critic is like the helpful guide who shows you just where you can get the best view of the object. Perhaps the object is a waterfall and you have to climb a thousand feet to the finest view of it. But the critic is not commanding you to climb. He is telling you a fact about your consummatory field, and if your drive is strong enough from your interest in the falls, it is a safe prediction you will find that observation point. You would, in fact, find it for yourself if your interest persisted, but if you follow the directions of the experienced guide it will save you some trouble and pains.

Now obviously this is not the end. It is only the beginning of the story of responsible aesthetic criticism. There are many things that need to be straightened out and amplified. Just what, in concrete detail, is the object of criticism? What, more precisely, constitutes relevancy? May there not be a considerable variance in the optimum response? May there not be alternative objects of criticism in response to a single aesthetic vehicle? Is the object of criticism ever exhaustively attained? Isn't it an extrapolated ideal towards which men's perceptions approach? To most of these questions I would with various qualifications give an affirmative answer.

But the big point to see is that in our description of the process of aesthetic criticism all such questions are open to intelligent treatment. They are questions of fact to be settled in terms of the evidence concerning the factual relations among the aesthetic vehicle, the successive perceptions of it, and the process of approaching aesthetic maximization in the object of criticism.

To summarize, I wish to take care of a few

obvious objections almost certain to arise. Am
I denying that commands are a source of
"ought's"? Certainly not. One common meaning
of "ought" refers to command. But what I am
calling attention to is the presence of another
sort of "ought" which we all must recognize as
having to do with certain natural selective systems. Whenever a single dynamic agent operates
on two levels at once so that, like means and
ends, the lower level is accepted or rejected in
terms of its relation to the upper level, then the
upper level acts as a norm for the selection of
lower-level activities. And then we have a descriptive "ought." We say that the lower-level
activities ought to conform to the selective norm.
We have such a norm in all purposive behavior
and in the maximizing processes of the consummatory field. These are natural norms and generate natural describable tendencies and oughts.
The emotivist leaping to the conclusion that all
"oughts" are open or concealed commands fails
to observe that there are natural norms generating ethical and aesthetic obligations open
to empirical verification. Not all "oughts" are
commands, and some factual situations are normative in action. That Breughel's *Winter* is
beautiful and ought to be richly appreciated is a

value judgment and is also most probably true. We have seen why.

The second objection that I want to meet is that if a person doesn't want to get the optimum response to the Breughel, and prefers his own interpretation, what sense is there in saying he ought to have some other perception? My reply is that if he prefers something short of the maximum in the consummatory field, we might look into his motives and see what is blocking his consummatory principle in this instance. If a hungry man refuses to eat, do we say he prefers hunger to satisfaction? We rather begin to inquire what other motive is blocking his hunger drive. So I would ask what would stop a person from seeking to maximize his potential satisfactions in a Breughel? There are, of course, many reasons. But even supposing great variability of consummatory response were found true of human responses to the Breughel, it would still be true for any one man's consummatory capacities in respect to the Breughel, and his natural tendency to prefer satisfactions to dissatisfactions, that he ought to make the most of his own peculiar capacities. Would even an emotivist deny a preference for increasing rather than decreasing satisfactions?

A third objection is almost the opposite of the second one. It is that such a description of the object of criticism as we have given does not state anything significant and consequently does not contain any source of aesthetic obligation. The description of the object of criticism simply states (so the objection runs) that this object is the optimum response to the vehicle. Whatever is the most pleasurable response to a physical object, that is the object of criticism, by definition. So, if a certain view of an ashtray makes it look like a Greek vase, or the sight of it brings up the memory of a wonderful evening with the nicest friends, then these are the object of criticism for the ashtray. For these are the maximization of the satisfactions derivable from the ashtray.

Indeed, on the theory of the object of criticism proposed (the objection continues) it is probable that all objects are aesthetic objects of great beauty. For cannot any object set off an aesthetic ecstasy under the right conditions? So, not only do all objects turn out to have dispositional properties of supreme beauty, but by the laws of chance over a sufficient time all perceivable objects as objects of criticism could be regarded as equally beautiful, since they would all appear to be dispositionally capable of this same supreme beauty. A child may find more satisfaction in a dish mop than in the most life-like doll. So a man in an appropriate mood may find a more ecstatic beauty in a rusty piece of tin than in Breughel's *Winter*. Whence the rusty tin, on the theory above propounded, is as beautiful as Breughel's *Winter*. All that is needed to appreciate it fully is the competent spectator!

Though I have embroidered the foregoing objection a bit and, I hope, laid it open to its own reduction to absurdity, yet there are men who are saying something scarcely any different. It is true, of course, that a man may be stimulated to ecstasy by a shimmer of light, a speck of dust in a sunbeam, or by nothing in the external environment at all. Fugitive aesthetic perceptions arise from all sorts of conditions and, for an aesthetically sensitized man, may be experiences of supreme beauty. A dream can be a thing of very great beauty. But this is not the problem which we set before ourselves, or which generations of grateful and curious men have been inquiring about. What critics and aestheticians have been grateful for, and curious about, are certain objects which, with some more or less well-understood qualifications, can be *relied upon* to produce deep and extended satisfaction. It is because these objects determine and guide certain tendencies for response and can be *relied upon*, with proper qualifications, to exhibit these tendencies that they have posed a problem and elicited inquiry. In some way these objects consistently control human response in the direction of great aesthetic satisfaction. It is the qualifiedly reliable control exerted by these objects that our theory undertakes to describe. Now, only a few objects in the world have this capacity of qualifiedly reliable control of aesthetic perceptions. We are directing our interest to these, for they are the objects men have properly prized greatly.

So, what is our reply to this last sweeping objection? The contention was that any object has the capacity of arousing ecstatic satisfaction, so that all objects, in terms of their theoretical capacities, are equally beautiful. Our answer is that only a few objects control the conditions of aesthetic response. This control is generated by the aesthetic vehicle and carried on in terms of funding and relevancy in respect to the stimulating pattern of the vehicle. The objection fails to distinguish between random-occurring fugitive aesthetic perceptions and those experiences controlled by the craftsmanship of artists through an aesthetic vehicle and through funding to the production of systems of verifiably relevant perceptions which are the objects of aesthetic criticism. The description of these objects being verifiable is true, or, if shown to be in error, false. And judgments of comparison concerning the greater or less satisfaction constitutive of such objects are also true, or, if shown to be in error, false. Accordingly, once more the judgment that Breughel's *Winter* is a thing of great beauty *can* be true, and it probably is true.

In short, since aesthetic judgments of objects of criticism are either descriptions of natural consummatory norms, or else comparisons of men's fugitive perceptions with these norms, such judgments may be true.

3

THE DYNAMICS OF THE MASTERPIECE

WE UNDERTOOK to show, in the preceding chapter, that a normative judgment about a work of art stating that it is an object of aesthetic worth could be regarded as a true or false declarative statement. It followed that we could truly assert that a person entering into the consummatory field of a work of great potential aesthetic value implicitly acknowledged the norm of an optimum experience of the work. For in entering the consummatory field he entered into a dynamic process originating in his own impulses and involving his total consummatory capacities. This process was shown to be a selective system by which a spectator acknowledged his own errors of consummatory perception in terms of the optimum consummatory response available to the stimulus or control object. I was particularly concerned to correct the pronouncements

of a current theory contending that value judgments are simply disguised wishes or commands
which cannot be true or false. To make my
point, I implicitly accepted the premise of the
value-judgment school that values are to be
identified with emotive impulses. This is the
interest theory of value, the modern descendant
of the traditional hedonistic or pleasure theory
of value. Roughly, the theory states that positive
value is to be identified with satisfactions such
as pleasure and conative achievement and neg-
ative value with dissatisfactions such as pain
and frustration. Aesthetic value is then regarded
as a certain qualified species of satisfaction—
namely, consummatory satisfaction.

According to this theory, it is generally
acknowledged that instrumental values are dependent on consummatory values. Given consummatory values, one can make true or false
statements about the means of attaining them.
But the consummatory values themselves were
thought to be outside the sphere of truth or
error. My point was that the factual normative
relation which is admitted to exist between
means and end exists also (though with a difference) within the consummatory field itself.
Within the consummatory field there is a tend-

ency to maximize satisfactions. The relation between a lesser and a greater consummatory satisfaction is not, however, a means-end relation. Nevertheless, the tendency is factually there. When a response in the consummatory area which lessens the available satisfaction is made, it is corrected as an error. It is an act that *ought* not to have been performed. And, consequently, the response productive of the maximum satisfaction available to the stimulus conditions is the natural norm for the consummatory field and the one that *ought* to be performed.

When the stimulus conditions consist of the vehicle or control object of a work of art, then the natural norm is the optimum consummatory response available through funding the relevant details of this control object. The object of criticism in the interest theory is, accordingly, the maximum quantity of consummatory satisfaction available from the relevant responses to the control object.

It happens, however, that the interest theory of value does not have an uncontested monopoly of the value theory field at the present time. The emotive-judgment view has a plausible case only in terms of the interest theory, and only when this theory is very superficially handled. But there are at least three other contemporary theories of value bearing on the aesthetic field which should receive equally respectful consideration. These are the organistic, formistic, and contextualistic theories of the subject.[1] How would these theories handle the object of criticism? For it would be my suggestion, where a number of equally adequate theories have alternative interpretations in a field, to consider each of these theories on its merits and hold them all in view for the fullest appreciation and understanding of the field. When they conflict in their judgment of a work of art, this is a fair indication of a deficiency in the work, and the nature of the deficiency is specified. When they are in harmony in their judgment, we have a significant confirmation of the worth of the work.

All four theories—the mechanistic, from which the interest or satisfaction theory of value emerges, the organistic, the formistic, and the contextualistic—can accept without major qualification the analysis of the work of art given in the first chapter. They would all be ready to distinguish among the vehicle or control object, the perceptions stimulated by it, and the object of criticism dependent on the concepts of relevancy and funding. But there would be considerable difference of emphasis on the relative importance of these factors for aesthetic value, and particularly in the determination of the content of value in the relevant details. This result shows that in the last analysis the content of the object of criticism and its value depend on the aesthetic theory and its presuppositions by which this object is analyzed and described. The adequacy of the judgment of the object of criticism is dependent upon the adequacy of the aesthetic theory through which this object is described. That does not mean that the ultimate critical judgment is simply a matter of theory. It is, from my observation, a matter of fact; but the judgment of the true value of a work can only be reached by way of theory, as with any other fact, and the more adequate the theory the more nearly true the judgment.

Now the point that I wish to bring out in this chapter is that with respect to these other three theories of aesthetic value, as with respect to the satisfaction theory considered in the previous chapter, the process of attaining the object of criticism is conceived as a dynamic process instituting a selective system. The goal of the process is accordingly a natural norm in terms of these theories, just as the optimum of consummatory satisfaction in reference to the control object constitutes a natural norm of aesthetic value for the interest theory. The strength of these theories lies in this very circumstance —namely, the factual evidence for the operation of these dynamic selective processes.

Let me begin with the organistic theory. The theory that a work of art (or, more precisely, the object of criticism) is an organic whole and that its value consists in its organicity, has a long tradition. Traces of it can be found in Plato and Aristotle. It was intensively developed by the nineteenth-century idealists. After an interval of reaction at the beginning of this century, it has had a sort of renaissance and in a number of qualified manifestations may be considered as perhaps the prevailing theory among artists and poets today. And many contemporary critics and aestheticians have been developing its implications. Among these may be mentioned I. A. Richards in his later writings, Bertram Morris, John Dewey in one phase of his treatment of art in his *Art as Experience,* and Andrew Ushenko.

Ushenko's field theory of the work of art and especially of its highest manifestation, the masterpiece, is essentially an organistic theory. He bypasses and somewhat disparages the satisfaction theory I developed in the last chapter in favor of an organistic theory of the content of a successful work of art. The point stressed is the observed objectivity of a masterpiece, and the fact that this objectivity is attained to a large extent by what we called in the first chapter the internal reference test.

You will recall the importance given to the concept of relevancy for determining the details of the content of the object of criticism. Two tests of relevancy were indicated, the stimulus test and the internal reference test. The latter is the factor stressed by the organic theory. It is usually admitted that the details organized by the internal reference test are emotionally charged, but the aesthetic value is not in terms of the intensity and unit quantity of satisfaction, but in terms of the degree of organicity. It is held that the aesthetic demand is for every detail to fit into its place, so that every detail of the work calls for every other detail to be just the detail it is and none other, and reciprocally. The result is called an organic whole. It follows that if any detail is altered or omitted it damages the whole. And the result is a certain specific sort of satisfaction coming from every little detail referring to other details which in turn refer back to the original details. A masterpiece achieves a sort of internal purposiveness, setting up demands which it continually satisfies within its own structure.

The result is the achievement of a high degree of objectivity when this process is successfully brought to completion. For every detail of the work verifies the expectation of every other detail.

These points are brought out with emphasis in the following quotations from Ushenko's *Dynamics of Art*: "In art context establishes a perspective, i.e., provides the beholder with an exclusive way of perceiving things. This means, on the one hand, that data which would be unrelated to one another outside the perspective appear to bear upon one another within the established context, and, on the other hand, that any irrelevancy is promptly discharged from the aesthetic experience as an accidental intrusion because it happens to be out of place within the perspective, i.e., because it is not tied up with the rest. We all know, in listening to music, how to turn a deaf ear to an accidental cough from someone in the audience. And the more absorbed we are in the composition, the better is the total aesthetic effect protected from disruption. . . .

"Contextual control that protects aesthetic experience from irrelevant importation by the beholder's private imagination can be treated similarly." And then later, "A masterpiece is a masterful creation. This means that a masterpiece can control the beholder's experience better than an inferior work of art. The artist is the master provided his work compels the beholder's perception and imagination to follow an antecedently prescribed course. By contrast inferior art may be said to be no more than a source of stimulation for the exercise of the beholder's own imagination. At its greatest the contrast is between entertainment, on the one hand, and great art, on the other. And the mark of entertainment is the subjectivity of the beholder's imaginative response. . . . The nature of the contrast gives the reason why art is superior to entertainment. The reason is not the amount of satisfaction—the sense of importance that we derive at a display of our own imagination in the medium of entertainment may be a great pleasure—but the understanding that our imagination is no match for that of a great artist. The moment we yield to a masterpiece we raise the imaginative level of our experience. We are ready to renounce our private contributions and follow the leadership of a Shakespeare or Beethoven because the superior power and quality of their imagination is intuitively evident." [2]

You note first Ushenko's emphasis on objectivity derived from contextual or internal relevancy, and second his somewhat disparaging treatment of entertainment or mere pleasurable satisfaction. The superiority, the higher worth of the masterpiece, comes from its imaginative control, its objectivity through contextual relevancy or the principle of the organic whole. That is to say, its aesthetic value is not primarily in terms of its emotional satisfaction, but in terms of the massiveness and firmness of its organic structure.

Now, the point I want to bring out is that this particular kind of value derived from imaginative control in following the references of details within an organic structure is a dynamic selective system, and designates in this way an object of criticism just as exactly as the maximizing of relevant satisfactions was shown to do in the previous chapter. In fact, Ushenko's whole book is in the nature of a demonstration of this conclusion. To what I have already said about the organic view, supported by the quotations from Ushenko, little needs to be added. For what the organicists point out is precisely a dynamic process which can get hold of a spectator's imagination, and which, once properly started under the guidance of a highly organized masterpiece, does not ever relax but directs the spectator's perception closer and closer towards an apprehension of the total organic experience available there. Even if the work is not a perfect organic whole, still it guides the perception to such an approximation of complete organicity as it is capable of attaining. And the judgment of its degree of deficiency from complete organicity is the critical judgment of its degree of aesthetic failure.

Ushenko uttered the crucial phrase which reveals the objective selective process. His phrase was: "The moment we yield to a masterpiece." * This exactly describes our experience when we are in the presence of a highly organic work. To be sure, there is an "if" in the process.

* Because I have selected passages from Ushenko's book which stress the organic process, I do not wish to leave the impression that he is unappreciative of other basic features of the aesthetic experience, such, for instance, as vividness.

If we do not "yield" to the masterpiece, it cannot, of course, perform its selective action upon our powers of perception. Similarly, if we do not turn on an electric oven, it will not bake our bread. But once "yield" to the organic structure of a masterpiece and the selective process carries us along, excluding subjective errors of irrelevancy and directing us towards the total organic whole so far as it is achieved by the artist—which in this organic theory is the object of criticism and the goal of the appreciative process.

And this is the main point I wish to make in the present chapter. Elsewhere you can find out, if you do not already well understand, what the organistic theory of art is. But here I merely want to demonstrate that the process of appreciation and evaluation of a work of art in the organistic theory is an objective process and in the nature of a selective system. It is the process of maximizing the organic structure relevant to the vehicle of a work of art. The dynamics of the process consists in the impulse-charged references of all the details of the work, and there is a specific and peculiar satisfaction that comes from all of these references' achieving mutual completion within an organic structure. But the

aesthetic value for the organicist does not derive from the satisfaction, but from the organicity of the references for which the satisfaction
is simply a witness and a pleasant corollary.*

I wish to bring out the same point with respect to the other two important theories of art
—the formistic and the contextualistic.

The formistic theory of art emphasizes
natural norms or forms which on the evidence
brought forward mold things into their shapes.
It calls attention to the fact that things in the
world are not indiscriminately shaped but di-
vide into distinguishable species and types. In
modern terms these may be regarded as states
of relative equilibrium or steady states. Things
tend to exist at or near the center of these states.
They are very clearly discernible in the states
of inorganic matter which we know as the enduring types of atoms and which constitute a
certain level of cosmic equilibrium. As we
ascend the scale of complexity among natural
forms to molecular structures and organic cells

* The dynamic force or sanction of the organic process in or-
ganicism becomes even stronger than made out in the text when
one realizes that this is a categorial feature of the organistic world
hypothesis. That is to say, in this world theory the organic process
is a basic causal process descriptive of the mode of operation of
world events. What we have been describing in the text is simply
the operation of this cosmic process in the area of aesthetic facts.

and the species of plants and animals, the variations from the central most stable norm admitting a relative but precarious stability become more and more frequent. The central stable norm thus constitutes a natural norm, with a capacity for durable existence and, among living forms, for continuance of life. Unstable structures are in the nature of natural errors and are either incapable of existence and break up as soon as formed or lead a very precarious life at the mercy of slight environmental change.

This concept of the stable form is clearly a description of a selective system. The very cosmic forces which produce the particular structures that come into existence also determine the stable states which act as norms for the durability of these structures. Consequently, the same forces which institute the norms of stability eliminate the unstable forms that come into existence. Thus the unstable forms acquire the status of natural errors in this context.

Now when we enter into the sphere of human activity and social institutions, then, literally, unstable forms become errors in the domain of values. For in the formistic view the natural norms of value are the stable states of social organization and personality structure. Here, as with the organistic view, pleasure and emotional satisfaction do not constitute value. The stable and well-adjusted personality and corresponding stable social structure constitute value. Pleasure and satisfaction are merely symptomatic of stable relationships. A well-adjusted personality in a well-adjusted social structure tends to be happier and less frustrated than an unstable person in an unstable society. Widespread happiness is a fairly reliable sign of stability and value but does not constitute value. For biologically the responses which tend towards adjustment and stability tend to become the pleasant ones, and those that tend to endanger life tend to become unpleasant. An animal that enjoyed things that endangered its life would not live very long. So it is the capacity to live that legislates over our pleasures and is normative of our actions and emotions, not the reverse.

This conception of value has many bearings on the area of aesthetic values. But I will mention only two. Clearly the norm of the stable personality, and that of the stable society, will be legislative over the forms of art. They lead respectively to the conception of the work of art as that which appeals to the interests of the well-adjusted personality and that which expresses the cultural ideals of an age.

The most striking feature of the first conception is that great art has a morale-building and therapeutic character. In this view, great art is a powerful moral agent for building up a rich and healthy personality; and a great work of art is an expression of an integrated personality with deep emotional insight. By a process of intuitive contagion, a spectator responds to the emotional and perceptive insight of the artist and, insofar as these are well integrated and healthy, the spectator's dispositions are molded towards deeper insight and better adjustment. Thus music and novels and pictures can often do more to form a personality than discursive instruction or persuasion or discipline.

It is not necessary that the work of art represent well-adjusted actions—generally it does not—provided only that the motivation is true to life and the consequences truly shown. There is an implicit comment which says, "This is the way life goes. Observe it, and take it to heart, so as not to be deceived." There is no better way of exhibiting the normal and well adjusted than by depicting the unstable and ill adjusted and their troubles.

Nor is it necessary that the artist be himself exceptionally well adjusted (any more than that a good doctor should be exceptionally healthy), so long as he is open to, perceptive to, and aware of the direction that leads to frustration and that which leads to stability. It may be true that artists as a class are relatively unstable and poorly adjusted. But their troubles may be precisely what makes them exceptionally sensitive to the conditions that lead to the stability and happiness which they themselves lack and crave. The one thing that a great artist can never be is a rigidly conventional man. The disparaging term "academician" is testimony to this observation. A man like Van Gogh, who craved health, had more insight into the sweetness of health and the emotional vitality supporting it than the whole company of prize-winning academicians of his day who are now long since forgotten.

That there is a natural tendency to maximize normality in the object of criticism in the sense of human vitality, stability and adjustment hardly needs further argument. It is a direct consequence of our biological origin.

And now let us consider the cultural application of formism as the expression of the ideals of an age. The school of cultural relativists to which many anthropologists and art historians belong adheres to this view. It springs from a base of formism, because a culture that has the stability to mold the ideals and customs of an age must represent a relatively steady state. A culture constitutes a species of society. And it is obvious that an art that expresses the interests and aspirations of a culture will appeal to the members of that culture. There develops accordingly a tendency for the most highly appreciated works of an age to be exceptionally expressive of the age. So, a culture is also a selective system instituting a natural norm which rules over the content of the object of criticism.

We have thus found natural norms for the object of criticism derived from the interest, the organistic, and the formistic theories of value. There remains to be considered the contextualistic theory.

According to the contextualistic theory of art, aesthetic value is the vividness of quality of an experience, and a work of art is an object designed to produce in the spectator an experience of exceptional vividness. The aesthetic experience is thus opposed in this view to practical experiences and to habit and routine which tend to dull the perception of the immediate quality of acts and objects.

Now, it is true that one must adopt the aesthetic attitude to acquire the aesthetic experience of qualitative intuition. But, once the attitude is assumed, then it institutes a selective system in co-operation with a work of art designed to produce vivid experiences. Moreover, the contextualist points out that the aesthetic attitude of qualitative intuition is the fundamental attitude for the apprehension of the immediate qualitative nature of things. Consequently, there is a dynamic psychological tendency to take on that attitude when practical urgency or the inertia of habit and custom do not impress the mind. It is the attitude of release from practical claims and from the imprisonment of habit and so springs up spontaneously in a free and untrammeled mind. In other words, a mind unencumbered by practical urgencies or habit or custom will spontaneously assume this intuitive attitude.

The analysis of the work of art according to this view is exactly like that in the interest view elaborated in the first two chapters. There is the vehicle or control object, the perceptions stimulated by it, the operation of relevancy and funding, the culmination in an object of criticism. The only difference is that the guiding principle of selection is not primarily satisfaction but the vivid realization of the immediate quality of an experience. And this is a dynamic process of selection for the contextualist, just as satisfaction is for the exponent of the interest theory.

Evidence is at hand, therefore, for natural norms or selective systems in terms of each of the four main aesthetic theories. All of these theories could agree as to the analysis of a work of art given in the first chapter—about the vehicle, the fugitive perceptions, funding, relevancy, and the object of criticism. Their differences arise over the nature of the content controlled by the vehicle and selected for funding and the evaluation of the object of criticism. They differ on the basis of their selective systems.

Let me repeat that the main purpose of this chapter is not to harmonize the differences between the claims of the several relatively adequate aesthetic theories of our time, but only to show that these all can accept the analysis given of the work of art and of a verifiably describable object of criticism. For all of them the object of criticism is something that can be described in true or false declarative sentences and can be discussed intelligently in terms of the evidence available.

Particularly I wish to point out that differences among the four views regarding the description of the object of criticism are differences bearing on the evidence in support of their theories of value and fact and are consequently (in theory at least) as open to cognitive solution in terms of the evidence as family differences within any one of these theories. Admitted that categorial differences between world theories are more resistant to cognitive solution than differences within the categories of a single world theory, still the solution is in terms of the evidence that can be brought forward. Even if the categorial differences among world theories and their respective aesthetic views should turn out to be purely linguistic (which I doubt), it would still be true that these differences would be resolved in cognitive terms and in terms of the evidence produced.

My purpose in this chapter was to show that in the last analysis the selection of details for the object of criticism depends upon the description of aesthetic value supported on the evidence of our most adequate aesthetic theories; and that for all four relatively adequate aesthetic theories of the present time, the object of criticism would be a describable and cognitively verifiable object.

But I do not wish to conclude this chapter with the impression that the various selective systems given priority by the four aesthetic theories are irreconcilable *in practical criticism*. Major discrepancies of judgment occur, usually among the lesser works of art. The masterpieces generally conform to the natural norms of all four theories. At the risk of fusing distinctions drawn among the four views, let me call attention to the following overlappings of the norms when they are not too precisely considered.

Begin with the maximizing of satisfactions. Satisfactions do not occur in a vacuum. They are satisfactions in something. In what, then? The interest theorists would generally agree: Why, of course, in qualities of immediacy. But what are qualities of immediacy but the content of the contextualist's norm, which the contextualist also would admit gives satisfaction to the beholder; and to a large extent the more vivid the experience the more satisfactory. But both of these views would be left with unorganized perceptions and a failure to recognize the cumulative process leading to the object of criticism if they did not accept the action of internal relevancy in relation to the vehicle. So there we encounter the integrating action of the organic whole. And the development of an organic whole communicable from spectator to spectator or artist to spectator would be impossible if there were not normal modes of perception determined by the natural norm of the biologically healthy individual and the customs of a stable social culture. For communication from one person to another depends upon some sort of stability so that the symbols will have a constancy of meaning either in terms of a normal response to environmental objects or in terms of normal conditioning to the steady conventions of society.

So, on a superficial level, all these natural norms co-operate towards the determination of the object of criticism. We note a tendency to maximize *satisfactions*, but in the presence of an aesthetic vehicle we note also that this tendency is of a sort directed towards the funding of relevant details and with an emphasis on the *vividness* of the details, their character for the *normal* cultivated man, and their *organic* relationships.

The problem of the objective nature of the object of criticism would melt away if all these four factors could be maximized at once without the excellence of one factor often costing something in the potential excellence of another. But this much, I trust, has at least come out of our discussion—viz., that the conditions of priority for these factors in relation to one another is a factual problem to be settled by the evidence as it comes in. For these factors represent natural norms of human response. They are selective systems, ways by which behavior corrects itself in certain types of situations. These ways are open to description and verification. They are, in fact, the ways of man's pursuit of the masterpiece.

4

THE CONTROL OBJECT, A VEHICLE OF
AESTHETIC COMMUNICATION

IN THE FIRST CHAPTER, we saw that the work
of art is not a single object but a nest of related
objects. These were discriminated as (1) the
vehicle or control object, (2) the perceptions
stimulated by the vehicle which are the objects
of aesthetic immediacy, and (3) the object of
criticism. The second and third chapters were
devoted to a description of the object of criticism and the way it selects and gathers up the
relevant perceptions originating in the vehicle.
Now I wish to describe more in detail the nature of the vehicle and the manner by which
it controls aesthetic perceptions and accordingly
makes possible the communication of aesthetic
experiences between artist and spectator, between spectator and spectator, and between
critic and critic.

The aesthetic vehicle has two essential char-

acteristics. It is the *stimulus* for the consummatory perceptions which are gathered up into the
object of criticism. It has also some mode of *permanence* which affords it a continued existence
between the moments of aesthetic perception it
stimulates.

If it were not for the relative permanence of
the vehicle, there would be no permanence in
the object of criticism, at least so far as repeated
human experiences of it are concerned. For the
stability of our perceptions of the relevant details of the work of art depend upon the stability
of the stimulating vehicle. Without the stability
of the vehicle, there would be no stability in the
object of criticism. And this is something of a
paradox to many minds when it first comes home
to them: the fact that the stability, objectivity,
and relative permanence of the perceptual qualities making up the object of criticism depend
upon the stability of a vehicle which possibly
intrinsically contains none of the perceptual
qualities constituent of the object of criticism.
As stated earlier, the object of criticism is a dispositional property of the vehicle. The character of the object of criticism is predictable from
the vehicle. But it is possible that none of the
features characterizing the vehicle also charac-

terize the object of criticism. The physical and chemical characters of a painted canvas, which is the vehicle for a painting as an object of aesthetic appreciation, may have nothing in common with the perceptual qualities of the painting.

So, it becomes important to ask just what are the characters of an aesthetic vehicle which render it a suitable object for the stimulation and stable control of the object of criticism? And what types of vehicle are there?

The stable control of the vehicle is performed by two quite different agencies. The one is a relatively permanent configuration of physical properties, such as canvas and pigments for a picture. The other is a relatively permanent pattern of human action or tradition, such as language for a poem.

The second agency itself is divisible into two groups. There are first those patterns of human action which have a biological origin. These are a man's capacities for visual and auditory discrimination, for emotional responses and motor adjustment, for learning and conditioning. These are man's sensory responses, reflexes, instincts, and instinctive techniques of acquiring skills. These are what go to make up the conception of the normal spectator. As pointed out in the last chapter, these are assumed, especially in the formist theory, to be raised to a maximum in aesthetic response. The spectator for the object of criticism is not the arithmetic average of a community, but the man with full human capacities of sensory and emotional response and motor adjustment and powers of learning. He is not a slightly color-blind and tone-deaf individual such as the arithmetic average would have to offer. He is a fully capable human being. Granted that the normal man, in this sense, is an ideal man, it is nevertheless a stable ideal from which deficiencies can be estimated and allowed for in critical aesthetic judgments. Just as a cripple or a poorly co-ordinated man will recognize the *superiority* of a better co-ordinated man in a sport involving a motor skill, so a less discriminating man when he comprehends what is involved will recognize the superior discrimination of a keener or more cultivated man in judgments involving such discriminations. Indeed, in these areas the selective action of the natural aesthetic norms will precipitate the judgment sooner or later, anyway. Just as the better co-ordinated man wins in the sport, anyhow, the judgment of the more discriminating man ultimately holds as indeed the more discriminating, when through time the judgment of a work of art becomes gradually confirmed and settled.

Part of the stability of the aesthetic vehicle, then, is to be attributed to the patterns of response characteristic of the normal spectator. And from now on, as actually has generally been the practice in aesthetic discussion, the normal spectator will be assumed; for the patterns of action expected of the normal spectator are constant for all works of art. For instance, a discriminatory ear is assumed for listening to any piece of music. Not that every work of art requires the finest sensory or emotional discrimination, but the artist and critic is at liberty to demand it, if the full appreciation of the work leads that way. *

It is the second sort of patterns of human action that require special attention in describing

* If it should turn out that there are a number of normal human types, based perhaps on different physical conformations, it would follow that works of art that would appeal to one type might not appeal to another. This would complicate human aesthetics but not alter the principle of selective action in terms of normal perception as developed by the formist. It would simply mean that there are several centers of stability for man. The instability of abnormal and unhealthy individuals at variance from these several centers would still be observable.

the aesthetic vehicle, because these are not constant for all works of art but vary from work to work. These are the patterns produced by social conditioning—namely, social convention and tradition. There is probably no aesthetic vehicle that does not depend for its stability in some degree upon tradition. For the most part (after recognizing the important contribution of normal human reaction) the stability of response to the aesthetic vehicle is the combined result of the stability of the physical properties of the vehicle and of a tradition it exemplifies. The relative proportion of the function each performs in maintaining the stability of the vehicle varies greatly from object to object. In the visual arts like painting and sculpture, the physical stimulus carries most of the burden. In literature, tradition carries most of it. In some instances (now rare), as with the songs and epics of the ancient bards, where no physical continuant existed at all but only the memories of the bards themselves, everything depended upon tradition.

On first thought one tends to think that the more a work relies for its stability on the permanence of the material of a physical vehicle, the greater will be its likelihood of permanence.

But this correlation is not borne out. We have more remains of Greek literature and in better condition than we have of their sculpture or architecture, for stone crumbles and after it falls nothing remains; but tradition is versatile and relies only a little on the particular black marks on which it rides, so that it leaps lightly from parchment to paper and from one paper sheet to another and so comes down intact over many centuries. As in Horace's famous line:

Exegi monumentum ære perennius

and Shakespeare's,

And thou in this shalt find thy monument,
When tyrant's crests and tombs of brass are
spent.

(Sonnet CVII)

Let us rapidly review some of the typical forms of the physical vehicle and their ways of stimulating relevant responses in a normal spectator.

The simplest for bringing out its essential relationships is that of the picture. The physical vehicle of a picture is a fairly durable material body, easily transportable, as a rule, with a smooth surface on which shapes are rendered with pigments of various sorts. Canvas, paper, or a thin board are the customary materials, but sometimes stationary surfaces such as the walls of caves or buildings are used. In a picture, the shapes drawn on the surface directly stimulate the spectator. All the shapes are simultaneously within the view of a spectator stationed at a suitable distance in a suitable light—the optimum location we were talking about in the second chapter. Theoretically the whole picture can be taken in at a glance, for all of its stimulating areas lie within a single perspective in the view of the spectator. Actually, however, as we have seen, it takes many looks at the painting, with many changes of the focus of the eye and of the attention, and much funding to take in all the details. Moreover, there may be more than one optimum point of perception, as in a Renoir where one enjoys the color modulations and brush work close to the canvas, but must find the forms depicted by standing a few feet away.

More of the aesthetic details are given by direct stimulation in a picture than in any other major art. And yet a great deal depends upon conditioning and convention. All the representative side of painting depends upon conditioning. And the style of space representation employed, especially in the rendering of depth and three-dimensional mass, depends upon convention. So tradition, even in painting, absorbs a great deal of the function of stable control of the perceptual object.

Turning to sculpture, and passing over relief sculpture whose physical vehicle functions much like the surface of a picture, we come to a type of work that cannot possibly be taken in at a glance. A statue in the round can only be apprehended as an integral aesthetic object after the funding of many different perspectives; for the spectator has to go around it and take it in from all sides. Moreover, much sculpture (many critics will say all the best sculpture) has, besides its visual qualities, tactual qualities. It requires for full appreciation that it should be tactually felt, or at least arouse memories of what it would feel like to pass the hand over its surfaces. Nevertheless, like a picture, a very large proportion of the aesthetic details of a statue come from direct stimulation by the physical vehicle.

Turning our attention to architecture, we encounter a still greater multiplication of distinct perspectives that have to be funded for the full appreciation of the object. For the spectator has not only to walk all around the object but to enter into it, and to walk all through it and survey its numerous chambers and the walls and furnishings of them all. And here there is also an augmentation of the contribution from convention in all that has to do with the utility of the building in relation to the social institutions of the age. But still, as with the picture and the statue, the appreciation of the work emanates from the direct stimulation of the vehicle. There is no intermediary stimulus object between the control object and the spectator.

All this is altered when we enter the domain of music. For here characteristically there is a performer who interprets for the appreciative auditor the work of the composer. In music the two functions of the vehicle are, in a way, divided between two vehicles. For the score is here the basic control object that gives durability to the work, but the performer is the main stimulus object who produces the sounds that are heard and appreciated. If one is concerned mainly with the function of stability and control and the lasting power of a piece of music, one considers the score as the essential vehicle of the work of art in music. But if one is thinking mainly of the stimulus function, one considers the performer as the vehicle. The absolutely essential thing is to realize that both functions are needed for the full functioning of the aesthetic vehicle in music and that in music these functions are divided between two different objects, the performer and the score.

If the physical vehicle is considered from the point of the stimulation due to the performer's instrument, then one thinks of the appreciated musical object, as with painting, to be something largely due to the source of direct stimulation. But then the steady durability of the work is lost sight of. On the other hand, if the composer's score is taken as the pivotal vehicle, then the situation is very much like that in the art of literature. For the score is just a succession of symbols to be read off by the musician, and the stability of these symbols depends upon the social convention which gives meaning to the symbols. The score, the social convention, and the physical performance of the musician are all usually needed for obtaining the appreciation of a piece of music.

A curious variation occurs with the highly skilled musician who can read a score off directly and obtain through his auditory imagery the sounds of the piece as vividly as if it were physically produced. I knew one such musician who rarely went to concerts, because, as he said, he could take up a score and read it off as he would like to hear it performed; whereas at a physical performance of it he was constantly bothered by renderings that were less than perfect to his ear.

A recent development in music is the phonograph record, which affords still another musical vehicle. By this means a particular performance may be given a permanent embodiment. If the record is taken as the musical vehicle, then the situation in this art is very close to that of the visual arts, where the physical vehicle directly presents all the sensuous stimuli for aesthetic appreciation.

If the phonograph record should come to be regarded as a terminal physical vehicle in music, the relationships of the original score to the record would be very much like those of the plans of a work of architecture to the finished building. The score would then be analogous to the architect's plans and elevations, the performance analogous to the work of the contractor and his crew under the direction of the architect, and the final record analogous to the finished building sensuously complete for the direct appreciation of the beholder.

But it is still customary to regard a phonograph record as a reproduction—something short of the original—like photographs of a building, or rather like the careful colored reproduction of a painting, not a terminal example of the work of art. The musical score is still customarily regarded as the pivotal vehicle. If we refer to Beethoven's *Fifth Symphony* as the work that has endured for appreciation through half a dozen generations, we think of Beethoven's score. This is the enduring vehicle that has been performed by hundreds of orchestras and of which we have several recorded interpretations by conductors of exceptional imagination and genius.

The musical vehicle brings to the fore a number of other aspects of the vehicle. There may be a number of genuine copies of it. The vehicle may be a multiple object. There are many copies of Beethoven's score. It has been carefully edited and printed by the thousands. Each printed copy of the score is an equally genuine copy of the original vehicle. It is the same, obviously, with any work of literature. A poem, in respect to its vehicle, is any well-edited, printed, or even written, copy of the poem. This is different from most paintings, statues, and works of architecture, although even among these are processes which give multiple vehicles. All instances of the graphic arts—etchings, lithographs, wood-block prints, photographs—are examples of multiple vehicles. So are casts of bronzes in sculpture. So might be prefabricated buildings, if some of these should rise above the level of mere commercial products. The physical vehicle of a work of art is not necessarily just one particular object. It may be a whole edition of objects.

Also, we must make an allowance for reproduction of a work of art, when these are relatively faithful copies of the original. These also have much authentic worth and owe their beauty, of course, mainly to the original artist and only secondarily to the skill of the reproducer or the perfection of the reproducing process.

Thirdly, we become acutely aware of the existence of alternative interpretations of an original work all equally relevant and equally beautiful, or very nearly so. In recent years much study has been made by able critics of the relevant ambiguities of a work of art. These are

alternative responses to a single stimulus element in an aesthetic vehicle. Often, indeed
generally, these alternative relevant responses
cannot be simultaneously had. They may be
funded, however, and the aura of one response can modify the experience of another in
process.

But sometimes the ambiguities are more
extensive than that. Alternative consistent interpretations of a work or of relatively integral
segments of a work may even exclude one
another. Consider the many interpretations of
Hamlet. An actor is, of course, a performer, and
his relation to an author's play is much like that
of a musical performer to a composer's score.
Shakespeare's Hamlet is a complex character.
One imaginative actor after another has developed a consistent personality out of him, but the
pattern of emphasis has varied from actor to
actor. The complexity of the character makes
a number of interpretations organically relevant.
Moreover, there is the typically theatrical problem of adapting the character to the physical
build and special potentialities of the actor. A
playwright with a view to many performances
of his play by diverse actors no doubt allows for
these interpretations. And it becomes a nice crit-

ical problem to judge where a performer has exceeded the limits. There is a point where an interpretation ceases to keep in contact with the original and becomes a translation. Some translations may be as beautiful as the original, and even more beautiful. But when the original is an object of exceptional beauty, this is rarely so. For a translation is not necessarily a rendering into another verbal language. It may be a converting into another set of artistic conventions, or its emotional tone may be altered. But a translation is no longer the original, and if it too is beautiful it must be appreciated as if it were a different vehicle producing a different object of criticism. It has been said that some of Gilbert Murray's translations of Euripides are more beautiful than Euripides' original plays. If so, these are really new plays, and Gilbert Murray is their author, and the new vehicles are the printed words composed by Gilbert Murray for which the source material was the plays of an ancient Greek author. The same result may be brought about by an actor or producer in English of an English play. The usual modern interpretation of the Jew in *The Merchant of Venice* may be more properly regarded as a translation of Shakespeare's play than as an interpretation.

It may indeed be better than Shakespeare's intention. According to some critics, the same is to be said of the modern interpretation of Falstaff in *Henry IV*, though I as a lay reader find this very hard to accept. But the principle that distinguishes a translation from an interpretation is clear enough. The former in important respects alters the original vehicle either by changing its physical stimuli (as notably by substituting the symbols of one language for those of another), or by abandoning the relevant responses to the stimuli and substituting others. An interpretation makes no such alterations. A translation is rarely as good as a conscientious interpretation of an original. And when the translation is definitely superior, it may well be regarded as a totally new work.

Having mentioned the theater, we are prompted to observe some of the peculiarities of its vehicle. Here we have a performance resulting from the co-operation of a large number of artists, each an expert in a particular function. Of course, an orchestral performance in music presents the same situation, but in the theater the complication of relationships is particularly obvious. There is first the dramatist who **writes** the play. There is then the theatrical director who develops his interpretation of the play and selects the actors and the stage designers and who supervises all the other technicians connected with the performance. Under the general guidance of the director's interpretation of the total intention of the play, each actor is expected to develop his interpretation of the character he is representing. The scenery and the lighting have to be similarly considered in their relation to the whole. It is a vast co-operative enterprise. When it is a first performance and the author is available to work with the director, it is not uncommon for the author to change his script as he sees the possibility of improvements that come to light in the process of actual performance. And (more dubiously) it is a common thing for a director to make cuts in a play, or even to alter certain lines (which if carried beyond a certain point converts the performance into a translation rather than an interpretation).

The performance of a play is such a complex enterprise that it comes near to being a fugitive art. And no way as yet has been found of making adequate reproductions of a theatrical performance anywhere approaching the faithfulness of a phonograph recording of a symphonic performance. Whatever permanence there is to the theater beyond the run of the play while the cast is held together comes from the playwright's written drama which is essentially a piece of literature.

The dance is an even more fugitive art, for as yet no thoroughly adequate choreographic symbolism has been found so that a complete dance can be preserved on paper as a piece of music can be, or a play. Where a dance endures, it is held mainly by tradition, passed from generation to generation. Since such traditions are the exception in our civilized society, it is mainly among primitive peoples and among surviving ancient cultures that we find an enduring dance. And perhaps I will not be gainsaid if I venture the opinion that the art of the dance is still at its greatest where such traditions persist— among primitive peoples or other groups retaining a firm and ancient tradition such as are to be found in many parts of Asia.

Let us take finally a glance at the vehicle of literature. This art is peculiar in having a physical vehicle that offers a minimum of sensuous stimulation. A novel or a poem is read directly by the person appreciating it, and ordinarily in silence. A poem may be read aloud, but rarely by an expert performer, and most of us prefer our own interpretations to the usual run of elocutionary performances that we may have been subjected to. In this art, almost all of us are like that musician I previously mentioned, who preferred to listen to a work in silence. Literature may be safely regarded as one of the arts that does without a performer. And yet the physical vehicle, the printed page, is the thinnest of all sensuous stimuli; and its appearance to the eye, though not entirely irrelevant, as the visual form of a poem with its indented lines indicates, is yet so slight a contribution to the quality of the aesthetic experience arising from it as to be almost negligible. Indeed, if a poem loses nothing by being read aloud, then the visual effect of its printed symbols may be totally neglected. Nevertheless, the quality of the aesthetic experience in literature is sensuously rich and vivid and as stable for communication between reader and reader (so far as evidence shows) as that obtained from a musical performance or a picture. Whence come the qualitative richness and stability of response?

The answer is, from tradition. From tradition and deeply implanted habit in acquiring the pronunciation and the meaning given to words in a cultural environment. From the earliest days of his appearance in the world, a child is surrounded with words and soon attains extraordinary skill in their use. There is never any letup in the increase and perfecting of this skill, particularly in one who comes to develop a special interest in words—the prospective writer or lover of literature. He becomes the exponent and representative of his culture in this respect, the carrier and the norm-giver of the sounds and meanings of its words. As the leader and preserver of the tradition, there is no wonder that he is understood by all that are drawn to listen to him out of the same tradition. Thus a very thin physical vehicle can carry a very thick tradition. And a man who is intimate with the linguistic tradition can, upon stimulation by a few words cunningly put together, obtain a sensuously vivid image, or emotional attitude, or conceptual message which will be surprisingly uniform for all discriminating men throughout the culture.

These remarks about a degree of uniformity of response to the aesthetic vehicle will lead naturally to the question of communication in the arts. The verbal symbol in practical discourse is the prevailing instrument of communication among men. It is widely assumed that practical discourse is limited to the communication of conceptual meanings—references to singular objects like Paul or Peter, to classes like "man," relations like "above" and "between," qualities like "sweet" and "blue," and to complexes of these. But practical discourse is just as seriously concerned with the communication of attitudes and emotions and even sometimes with the unique quality of an event.

A salesman is unquestionably a very practical man. His practical aim, however, is to soften sales resistance, to generate an emotional attitude in his client. As we commonly say, the salesman communicates his enthusiasm for the article to his client. We say "communicates" whether the salesman down in his heart feels the same enthusiasm for the article or not, though I have heard it is a part of good sales technique for the salesman to build up in himself a belief in the virtues of the article he is promoting. He thereby communicates by a sort of contagion. Of course, he also arouses the attitudes he desires by causing his clients to have apprehensions for their health or even their lives if they fail to purchase the article. Or he brings in the motive of keeping up with the Joneses next door who already possess the article, and plays on the envy and insecurity of his client—and so on. The salesman is trained in the techniques of arousing and communicating these emotions and attitudes, and with proper qualifications the effectiveness of these techniques is predictable. If it were not predictable, he would not make a living as he does and, frequently, so it would appear, a very good one.

Now, I mention the salesman and his techniques so as to dispose of a widespread notion disseminated by some of the excessively conceptually-minded philosophers to the effect that emotions and attitudes and even sense qualities, being private occurrences in the minds or hearts of individuals, are incommunicable. If they can be controlled and predicted by suitable techniques, obviously they are predictable and so also communicable. Not only every salesman, but every politician, lawyer, minister, doctor, and teacher when he seeks to be persuasive as well as merely informative, controls in predictable ways these supposedly private and incommunicable entities. And so does the artist.

The crux of the matter is, of course, not communication but control. Communication, however defined, is a special instance of control. At just what point does control of emotions pass over into communication? A doctor, wishing to induce in his patient a concern about the seriousness of a disease and the importance of following a regimen, does not himself necessarily feel the same serious concern over the disease that he wishes the patient to feel, since it is not he who has the disease. Yet it is definitely the physician's intention to induce a particular emotional attitude in the patient, and an experienced physician will know the techniques to employ to produce this effect. If successful, the physician has transmitted something. Colloquially we say that he has got his intention across. And yet the intention of stimulating a certain attitude in the patient does not consist in setting up in the patient's mind an attitude identical with that in the physician's mind. Is this an instance of communication?

Or must emotional communication involve something more—namely, the implanting in one mind of an attitude identical or nearly similar to an attitude in another mind? In the communication of ideas, we are likely to assume that the communicating symbols arouse identical ideas in the two minds concerned. Yet it is doubtful if that often occurs. And what of deliberate deception, where the intention is to implant an idea in another's mind which one does not have oneself; or of commands, when one gets another to obey in doing something one does not intend to do oneself; or of discussion in which the intention is to help ideas grow and to stir up an idea in another's mind not yet appearing in one's own? Are these or are these not communication? There is a graded series from stimulation of an idea without transmission—as when the alarm goes off in the morning to remind you of an early appointment—to apparent transmission of an identical idea from one mind to another, as with mathematical expressions such as $2 + 3 = 5$.

And so too with the control and communication of emotions and attitudes. At just what point shall we say control without communication passes over into communication proper? All that I am pointing out just now is that the important thing in the relation of a work of art to the spectator is control, and that communication is a special sort of control usually regarded as involving some degree of similarity of content between the point of origin and the point of termination of the act of communication.*

Now, theoretically, the vehicle of a work of art could control the spectator's perceptions, without the artist ever having had those perceptions at all. The artist might simply know the techniques that would produce the desired effects and accordingly apply them. Some actors use that method. And an actor playing a highly emotional role night after night in a long continuous run could not possibly (or, surely, only in the rarest instances) take on the emotional intensity in his body every night that he hopes to induce in his audience. Within limits creditable aesthetic effects of control through the vehicle of a work of art can be obtained without communication in any strict sense between artist and spectator.

And yet the communication theory of art production has a strong hold. There is probably a

---

* Actually the problem of communication is even more involved than the text indicates. I have been writing in the tacit assumption of what may be called the *vehicular theory* of communication, which presupposes the transmission of closely similar content from one mind to another. But an *operational theory* of communication is possible which does not presuppose similarity, and conceives the communicative act rather like that of two persons on a teeter-totter. There is also a *coherence theory* of communication. But I am not troubling the reader with these.

very good reason that it has. It amounts to this, that there just does not exist any other reliable technique for the production of a masterpiece than that of the artist himself feeling and experiencing the perceptions which are to be funded in the object of criticism. The delicate balance of relationships in establishing organic relevancies and the precision of stimuli required just cannot be obtained in any other way. By means of his artistry and his sensitive acquaintance with the cultural symbols of his day, an artist feels his way towards a vivid and satisfying consummatory experience. When the physical vehicle that he has created returns to him the experience that he has been working for, he lets it stand as finished. The vehicle can then arouse this experience in him again, and can arouse it in other equally discriminating individuals.

Because the vehicle has this power of rearousing former experiences, it can be regarded as a symbol for them and as an instrument of communication. Undoubtedly an artist often intends the vehicle to perform this function. But sometimes, without much question, he is thinking not of other people but simply of giving expression through some physical vehicle of an intense emotion that is demanding an outlet. The vehi-

cle then reveals the artist's experience uninten-
tionally and gratuitously.

One suspects that most of the finest works of
art have been produced in a sort of middle state
between pure expression and a desire to share
experiences with others. Pure expression for expression's sake may lead to technical carelessness
and a vehicle that does not precisely control its
responses. Too much concern for the sharing
with others can lead to the demoralizing tempta-
tions of popularity. The best result probably
comes when the artist becomes absorbed in the
expression for its own sake but feels that it is so
fine and significant that he wants everybody else
to share it with him.

The aesthetic vehicle, then, may suitably be
regarded as a symbol for the communication of
consummatory experiences. It is not, however, a
mere symbol for communication. It is primarily
an instrument for control of aesthetic experience
and secondarily a symbol for communication.
The communicative function is best regarded
as a corollary of the control function, however,
else we get some unnecessary restrictions upon
aesthetic theory and criticism, such as the notion that an artist's intention should determine
the final judgment of a work. A work may con-

tain some happy accidents, and an artist does not always know all that he has put into his work.

One more point on the score of communication. There are many who believe that conceptual meanings can be precisely communicated but that emotions, attitudes, and sensuous immediacies which make up a great part of the content of art cannot. And then there are others who believe that a highly organized work of art communicates or controls the aesthetic response with great precision. I incline to the latter view.

One must not ask of aesthetic communication more than one does of practical and scientific communication. People often misunderstand each other in practical and scientific discourse, to say nothing of philosophical discourse. It is only the most successful aesthetic vehicles that should be compared with the most precise conceptual forms. Also one must remember that only those who understand a conceptual language can obtain a precise communication through it. The same is true of aesthetic vehicles, which also depend on cultural tradition and, besides, upon the acquisition of fine sensuous and emotional discrimination. It may easily be conceded that an aesthetic vehicle can never attain to the precision of control over response and communication that an equation in physics can. Its main function is consummatory richness rather than unequivocal precision. But the aesthetic vehicle of a highly organized masterpiece may well exceed in precision of communication a sociological analysis of a cultural conflict or a psychological analysis of a type of neurotic personality, where the subject matter approaches the emotional richness and internal complexity of that of a work of art.

I am simply pointing out that whereas not every aesthetic vehicle is precise in its powers of aesthetic communication, neither is every scientific statement. But both appear to have great capacities of control over response when properly constructed and when responded to by persons who have acquired the expected discrimination, or, if you will, have learned the language.

And now one final point. Since it is control of a type of response that distinguishes the aesthetic vehicle rather than an intention to communicate, it follows that natural objects may also be aesthetic vehicles. There are classics of nature —Yosemite Valley, Niagara Falls, Mount Rainier, Lake Tahoe, Point Lobos. Our society has come to recognize their aesthetic significance in the institution of state and national parks for the preservation of natural beauty. And there are multiple objects of beauty in nature, such as seashells, snowflakes, flowers, and birds—and sea waves, and lichened rocks, and (why not add?) sunsets. These as natural vehicles of beauty are what etchings and wood blocks are as fabricated vehicles of beauty. And we could have just as much to say about these as about the control objects of the arts. Too little, in fact, has been said about natural beauty in recent decades. It is strange that in an epoch when more attention is being given to natural beauty by the general public than ever perhaps in the history of man, less attention is being given to it by critics and aestheticians than at almost any other time. There are whole schools of aestheticians that limit their field to the arts, and some who tolerantly concede that people become aware of a beauty in nature only through a borrowed light as a reflection from the arts of man.

But I cannot expand here on this provocative theme. Let me only suggest, by all that we have described as the control object and aesthetic vehicle of the arts, that natural objects are just as truly control objects and aesthetic vehicles provided only that they induce responses having the character of aesthetic value. What that character is we have discussed already. And almost in the same sense that an art vehicle may be a source of communication of aesthetic quality from one man to another, so may a vehicle of natural beauty. Just as sometimes the best way I can conceive of communicating an attitude I feel to another is to play in his presence a piece on the piano, or to send him a poem in which the poet has caught the mood I want him to sense, so I might send him a maple leaf autumn-turned, or a blossom, or I might point to a hummingbird poised before a flower, or perhaps stand with him silently by the beating surf, or before the silver path of the moon on a still lake.

5

A REPLY TO EXTREME RELATIVISTS IN CRITICISM

EARLIER IN this book we met an objection to our mode of describing a work of art to the effect that value judgments were neither true nor false. We pointed out that this objection was based on an arbitrary identification of value judgments with commands and wishes, and that it failed to take account of certain factual relationships constituting the work of art which are as open to description and to verifiable judgment as any other rather complex factual relationships. The vehicle, the perceptions stimulated by the vehicle, the funding process, and the selective systems determining the field of relevant traits as a dispositional property of the vehicle, are all matters of fact open to description by a discriminating observer. By a trick of definition—by defining the aesthetic judgment as a kind of command rather than a kind of factual statement

—the emotive-judgment school evades this group of facts. The facts, of course, remain in spite of the evasive definition. And that is why I believe the tenets of this school will not prove formidable in the long run. Facts have a way of speaking for themselves.

But there is another objection by another school of aestheticians which needs to be taken much more seriously, because this one refers to the facts. This is the objection of the so-called relativists, who declare that there is no determinate judgment regarding the nature and value of a work of art valid for all men or for all cultures. The nature and worth of a work of art alter from culture to culture, from man to man, possibly even from momentary perception to momentary perception. The relativists of this school do not deny that judgments about the character and value of a work of art may be true. But they are true in some highly-restricted or variable sense.

The initial difficulty with the relativists is to find out just what they mean. One relativist differs from another in the mode of his insistence on relativity. Of course, even the view developed in this book requires some relativity. The judgment of an object of criticism is relative to the existence of a vehicle and the responses of a normal discriminating spectator. In the nature of the factual relationship described these could probably only occur in human society. Our view is thus relative to man. But our view does entail the possibility that a true judgment of the character and value of an object of criticism can be made which would be true irrespective of the perceptual limitations of particular spectators, and irrespective of the failure of the object to conform to the particular cultural pattern of the critic. It is such extreme relativists as seem to deny even this much objectivity of aesthetic judgment who require serious attention before we take leave of the subject before us. Perhaps there is no better way of summarizing emphatically the position taken in these essays than by contrasting it with the position of the more restrictive relativists.

Let us take, then, the view of some prominent relativist in the aesthetic field and examine his arguments and his evidence for them. I can think of no better man for this purpose than George Boas. His brilliant book with the ironic title *Wingless Pegasus* offers an authoritative exposition of a rather extreme form of relativism. Its terminal essay, "The Mona Lisa in the History of

Taste," which first appeared some years earlier, has become a sort of classic for aesthetic relativism. I shall restrict my attention mainly to this essay. For here the issue between my position and his can be squarely faced in the treatment of a specific well-known work of art.

He begins his essay with this challenging statement: "The search for aesthetic standards by means of which any work of art can be finally judged would seem to presuppose either that every such work is an unchanging entity, or that, regardless of whether it changes or not, it should always be judged in the same way. Neither of these presuppositions appears tenable to the writer of this paper, who holds, on the contrary, that works of art are not the locus of one value known as 'beauty' or something similar, but are rather multivalent, that certain of their values are experienced by some persons, others by others, and that there is no a priori method—except that of fiat—of determining which of the many values are properly 'aesthetic.' "

To see more specifically what Boas means by "multivalence" we may look at an earlier passage in the book from a section headed "Multivalence": "Not only may a thing or process have both instrumental and terminal value, but it may at the same time have several kinds of each. Eating is both useful for preserving life and also a pleasant pastime. The meal which one eats is a means of a cook's earning his living, or a host's entertaining his friends, of his friends meeting together for conversation, of a series of voluptuous tastes, sights, and smells, and so on. A book, let us say *Pickwick Papers,* may be useful to a reader who wants to know something about manners and customs in early nineteenth century England, who wants to pass an examination in English literature, who has a lecture to give on English humor; it may also and at the same time be very amusing just to read, as indeed it is, and be read for no purpose ulterior to the amusement which is in it. Writing it may have been a pleasant occupation for Dickens, and at the same time an economic necessity. In fact, the inherence of a large number of values in anything would be obvious if theorists had not decided that one must forget most of them. But if one does not arbitrarily excise certain of the values as irrelevant, one is forced to the conclusion that anything may and usually does satisfy several interests."

This second quotation makes it clear that the

multivalence Boas has in mind applies mainly to what we have been calling the vehicle of the work of art. No one, of course, could seriously deny that the physical vehicle of a work of art could be used, and often is used, for a great variety of purposes. Boas' list of uses is the merest beginning. A copy of *Pickwick Papers* could make a good paper weight, a source of fuel in an emergency, a weapon of attack if nothing heavier were at hand. But such values are clearly distinguishable from certain other values derivable from a physical copy of *Pickwick Papers,* notably from certain terminal values.

Just previous to the passage quoted, Boas has been at some pains to distinguish terminal from instrumental values. He does not give the impression of regarding this distinction as arbitrary, or a priori, or a matter of mere fiat. It appears to be a distinction forced upon a careful observer by the facts. And when an object formerly valued as an instrument comes to be valued as an end, this is apparently for Boas a notable occurrence. He even slips (if it is a slip) into calling the terminal value "beauty." "But the most impressive evidence of the emergence of terminal from obsolete instrumental values," he writes, "is found in museums, such as that founded in Dearborn by the late Henry Ford, in which people simply look at all kinds of instruments, carriages, sleighs, furniture, lamps, which were all made for use, not primarily for beauty. *Their beauty has arisen from the obsolescence of their utility*" (italics mine).[1] There seems to be nothing arbitrary or a priori in the observation of this distinction, nor in the exclusion of utility value from the value given these objects by visitors to the museum in Dearborn. Nor does there seem to be anything illegitimately arbitrary for Boas, according to this passage, in naming this value "beauty" any more than in naming it "terminal," which Boas never gives any intimation of considering arbitrary. And let me interpolate here incidentally that one of the common conceptions of aesthetic value, or beauty, consists precisely in its identification with what Boas is here naming "terminal value."

If one appreciates the significance of this point—that the distinction between instrumental and terminal values is not a matter of arbitrary fiat but an observation of an empirical difference of fact, and that the naming of the terminal value with the symbol "terminal" or even with the symbol "beauty" is not arbitrary in any sense other than the selection of a name for a class of distinguishable responses—then one can easily see that any other empirical distinctions observed among values will not be arbitrary either. That is, the naming itself is significant evidence that Boas makes an objective distinction here between two kinds of value. Boas himself mentions the possibility of a number of kinds of terminal values also. If a writer elects to name one of these species of terminal value, rather than the whole genus, "beauty," that would be his privilege and would not be arbitrary in any empirically illegitimate sense, either. The only requirement is that the writer recognize the observable relations between the species of value he is attending to at the moment and other species. And the same with any other empirical distinction found among values.

What, then, would be illegitimately arbitrary for an empirical writer in aesthetics? It would have to be something, I suppose, that had the effect of distorting the evidence. An appeal to a priori certainty or self-evidence for some definition of beauty, I would agree with Boas, would be an instance of this, or a dictatorial insistence by personal fiat for a definition of beauty for which no justifiable evidence is offered. I would

also agree with Boas that a good many aestheticians in the past have been guilty of these
forms of arbitrariness. But what is there of an
a priori nature or of irrational fiat in the description of observable distinctions among values
and the concentration of interest upon some
one distinguishable species of value that can
suitably in conformity with usage be called aesthetic? Nothing, of course. So what leads Boas
into this false dilemma of positing either no
distinguishable aesthetic value and only an in-
discriminate multivalence, or else arbitrary fiat
and the a priori?

The answer is his failure to carry out first an
empirical study of the complex nature of a work
of art. In common with most writers on aesthetics he accepts the work of art vaguely as
some single object of reference. He does not
clearly distinguish between the physical vehicle, the perceptions stimulated by it, and the
object of criticism as a dispositional property of
it. The first is obviously multivalent like all
physical objects in that it is capable of many
uses. The second, any one particular perception
of the vehicle, is usually univalent. Any particular perception is usually in response to some
particular use or mode of enjoyment of a physi-

cal object. The third is univalent in the sense that it is generated by a specific sort of selective system which is commonly called aesthetic—such, for instance, as the maximizing of consummatory satisfactions. This mode of selection is empirically observable, as we have seen, and is no more arbitrary than any other natural selective process, no more arbitrary than the flow of water in brooks and rivers forming the drainage system of some valley. The multivalence of the physical object which serves as the vehicle of a work of art is thus quite consistent with the univalence of the object of criticism which determines the aesthetic worth of a work of art.

This statement is somewhat oversimplified, of course, as we know from our detailed study of the object of criticism. The description of the selective system determining the structure and worth of an object of criticism is not as easy to work out as that determining the flow of water in a valley. And a candid observer must concede that there is a lot yet to be learned about the process. There are several alternative theories stressing different factors in the process—one stressing satisfactions, another organicity, another stability, and another vividness. These are different theories about the selective process interpreting the evidence now available in different ways.

It would appear from a number of Boas' remarks in *Wingless Pegasus* that he confuses these alternative hypotheses about the selective process and the resulting nature of the object of criticism with the multivalence of the physical object serving as the vehicle of the work of art. The various instrumental and terminal values which may be attached to the physical vehicle of a work of art are, of course, taken as observed facts, not as a variety of descriptive theories about a fact. But the alternative hypotheses about the selective process generating the object of criticism are precisely this sort of thing—a variety of descriptive theories about a fact. It might be true that there are a number of selective processes generating a corresponding number of distinct objects of criticism. But it would still be important to distinguish among a number of different values as facts and a number of different theories about some one of these values. I incline to believe, however, until more conclusive evidence appears to cause me to change my mind, that there is only one ultimate process of selection of relevant traits for a work of art and that this process generates usually only one object of criticism for a given aesthetic vehicle.

Now, let us return to the essay on the *Mona Lisa*. We have so far found that Boas' opening statement expressing his extreme relativistic view of the multivalence of a work of art is initially plausible only because of its ambiguities and vagueness. In the light of our previous analysis, we can see that he confuses the physical vehicle with the object of criticism, ascribing a multivalence which, with qualifications, does truly apply to the vehicle, also to the object of criticism, to which it does not similarly apply. The physical vehicle can have all kinds of values, instrumental, sentimental, moral, and cognitional, as well as those ordinarily called aesthetic, and still be in its physical properties entirely neutral to them all. But the object of criticism by its very mode of generation is primarily an object of what is ordinarily called aesthetic worth; and, if any other sorts of value attach to it also, these are purely secondary and incidental.

And in Boas' opening statement of the *Mona Lisa* essay there is also implicit another confusion that becomes explicit in other parts of his book—the confusion between a variety of values that can in fact be attached to a single object and a variety of hypotheses that can be offered as descriptions of a single value process.

Let us hold these confusions in mind and proceed with the argument of his *Mona Lisa* essay. After the statement quoted earlier to the effect that "works of art are not the locus of one value, known as 'beauty' or something similar, but are rather multivalent," he calls attention to two objections often raised against his type of theory. The first is the argument from the classics that ". . . there happen to be some works of art which 'the judgment of posterity' has always held to be admirable or 'great,' and that one has only to examine their characteristics to discover what the distinguishing marks of great works of art are." The second is the argument that ". . . the work of art as the artist intended it is the real work of art. . . ." Boas briefly states the difficulties in finding an artist's intentions and the consequent fact that the work of art ". . . gives us only the slenderest clues to appropriate standards for judging it." He then drops the second argument as not worthy of more attention (to which I would on the whole agree), and proceeds to the body of his essay which is a scholarly effort to demolish the evidences for the first argument. In fact, Boas goes further than that. He not only undertakes to demolish the classic but evidently also intends to demolish the object of criticism which would unquestionably be "the locus of one value, known as 'beauty' or something similar," for he emphatically asserts that "works of art are not the locus of one value . . ." etc. Our two views, consequently, clash head on at this point. So let us follow the steps of this argument.

It is an argument from the evidences of men's reports on their judgments of the *Mona Lisa* from the time it was painted by Leonardo between 1503 and 1506 to the present day. It is an argument from the discrepancies of these reports in comparison with one another.

"The purpose of this paper," writes Boas, "is to take one of the works of art which have been most admired until recent times, and to examine briefly what critics or commentators of different periods have said about it. From what they said we hope to be able to infer what they were looking for. We are not so much interested in knowing why they admired the work of art as in knowing what they saw in it. It will be found that in at least this one case the work of art was identical with itself throughout history in name only."

Parenthetically, Boas seems to have over-stepped his main thesis of multivalence here, possibly to gain dramatic effect by exaggerating the paradox. He says he intends to leave us only with the *name* of the *Mona Lisa*. Even the physical vehicle is to lose its identity. You will find that *Pickwick Papers* was earlier allowed to be "an economic necessity" and "a valuable source of income," presumably the printed book that was, and is, bought and sold, not *only* the name. I am quite sure Boas does not intend to abolish the physical identity of the vehicle. As he says in one place, "But in general the physical appearance of works of art is fairly stable," which here allows for even a good deal of sensuous identity—the colors, for instance. But there is no question that Boas is demolishing the identity of the object of criticism, and anything similar—that is, trying to.

There appears to be little but the barest factual comment on the *Mona Lisa* till Vasari's enthusiastic report in 1550, forty years after it was painted. Boas points out that Leonardo's contemporaries would not have regarded it as his most important work. But Vasari praises it highly for the technical skill it shows and for its faithfulness to life, its realism. Here is the passage from Vasari quoted by Boas:

"Whoever shall desire to see how far art can imitate nature, may do so to perfection in this head, wherein every peculiarity that could be depicted by the utmost subtlety of the pencil has been faithfully reproduced. The eyes have the lustrous brightness and moisture which is seen in life, and around them are those pale, red, and slightly livid circles, also proper to nature, with the lashes, which can only be copied as they are with the greatest difficulty; the eyebrows also are represented with the closest exactitude, where fuller and where more thinly set, with the separate hairs delineated as they issue from the skin, every turn being followed, and all the pores exhibited in a manner that could not be more natural than it is: the nose, with its beautiful and delicately roseate nostrils, might be easily believed to be alive; the mouth, admirable in its outline, has the lips uniting the rose-tints of their colour with that of the face, in the utmost perfection, and the carnation of the cheek does not appear to be painted, but truly of flesh and blood: he who looks earnestly at the pit of the throat cannot but believe that he sees the beating of the pulses, and it may be truly said that this work is painted in a manner well calculated to make the boldest master tremble, and astonishes all who behold it, however well accustomed to the marvels of art. Mona Lisa was exceedingly beautiful, and while Leonardo was painting her portrait, he took the precaution of keeping some one constantly near her, to sing or play on instruments, or to jest and otherwise amuse her, to the end that she might continue cheerful, and so that her face might not exhibit the melancholy expression often imparted by painters to the likenesses they take. In this portrait of Leonardo's on the contrary there is so pleasing an expression, and a smile so sweet, that while looking at it one thinks it rather divine than human, and it has ever been esteemed a wonderful work, since life itself could exhibit no other appearance."

Then Boas notes that for a hundred years there is little or no mention of the *Mona Lisa.* The picture was, to be sure, in the French king's collection, but, whatever the reason, there is no critical reference to it. In the middle of the

seventeenth century it is mentioned by Père
Dan in a catalogue of the works of art at Fon-
tainebleau as "premier en estime, comme une
merveille de la peinture."

Just a little later comes the following comment
by André Félibien (quoted by Boas), still prais-
ing the technique and commenting on the
sweetness of the lady represented:

"This is one of the most finished of his works.
It is said that he took so much pleasure in working on it that he spent four months on it, and
that while he was painting this lady there was
always someone near her who sang or played
some musical instrument, so as to keep her joy-
ful and prevent her from assuming that melancholy air which comes over one easily when one
is inactive and motionless.

"Truly, said Pymandre, if I may give my opinion, the time which he put into it was well
spent, for I have never seen anything more finished or more expressive. There is so much
grace and so much sweetness in the eyes and
features of this face, that it appears to be alive.
When one looks at this portrait, one would say
it was a real woman who takes pleasure in being
seen.

"It is true, I replied, that Leonardo appears to have taken particular care to finish it well. And Francis I considered this picture to be one of the most finished products of this painter, wished to own it, and paid four thousand *écus* for it."

Then there appears to be no noteworthy criticism of the picture until the romantics of the nineteenth century, who bring in a new element. ". . . Gautíer and Pater . . . ," writes Boas, "both started a tradition—in apparent independence of each other—which has not died even today." Pater's passage is so well known that Boas only lifts out a sentence or two, but here is Gautier's description as quoted by Boas:

"Leonardo da Vinci retained the finesse of the Gothic period while animating it with a spirit entirely modern. . . . The faces of Vinci seem to come from the upper spheres to be reflected in a glass or rather in a mirror of tarnished steel, where their image remains eternally fixed by a secret similar to that of the daguerreotype. We have seen these faces before, but not upon this earth: in some previous existence perhaps, which they recall to us vaguely. How explain

otherwise the strange, almost magic charm which
the portrait of Mona Lisa has for even the least
enthusiastic natures? Is it her beauty? Many
faces by Raphael and other painters are more
correct. She is no longer even young; her age
must be that loved by Balzac, thirty years;
through the subtle modelling we divine the be-
ginnings of fatigue, and life's finger has left its
imprint on this peachlike cheek. Her costume,
because of the darkening of the pigments, has
become almost that of a widow; a crêpe veil
falls with the hair along her face; but the expression, wise, deep, velvety, full of promise,
attracts you irresistibly and intoxicates you,
while the sinuous, serpentine mouth, turned up
at the corners, in the violet shadows, mocks you
with so much gentleness, grace, and superiority,
that you feel suddenly intimidated, like a
schoolboy before a duchess. The head with its
violet shadows, seen as through black gauze, ar-
rests one's dreams as one leans on the museum
railing before her, haunts one's memory like a
symphonic theme. Beneath the form *expressed,*
one feels a thought which is vague, infinite, *in-
expressible,* like a musical idea. One is moved,
troubled, images *already seen* pass before one's
eyes, voices whose note seems familiar whisper

languorous secrets in one's ears; repressed desires, hopes which drive one to despair stir painfully in the shadow shot with sunbeams; and you discover that your melancholy arises from the fact that la Joconde three hundred years ago greeted your avowal of love with this same mocking smile which she retains even to-day on her lips."

Nothing said here about Leonardo's skill or fidelity to nature but much about a mysterious charm in the sitter and something deeply emotional if not sinister in her smile. Many other writers of this period discover these characteristics in the *Mona Lisa* or follow the leadership of those who first did. It is also noticed that the same smile is to be found in many other figure paintings of Leonardo, and many writers think they see a resemblance in the faces. Boas fails to see a resemblance in the faces but admits the similarity of the smiles, belittling the observation, however, as no more significant of emotional depth than the identity of the smiles of the archaic maidens in the Acropolis Museum in Athens. "Are we to conclude from this," he suggests, "anything except that such smiles were the fashion of the times." [2]

The next accretion of interpretations of the *Mona Lisa* in Boas' account comes in the twentieth century with the Freudians, beginning with Freud himself in his study of Leonardo da Vinci. Freud's interest was, of course, not primarily aesthetic but clinical or, rather, in the nature of an analysis of a personality structure. His conclusions are necessarily inferential on the evidence of what is known of Leonardo's life and what has come down to us of his writings and paintings. This evidence is reviewed by Freud in the light of his psychoanalytical experience to reach certain conclusions about Leonardo's character and the drives motivating his production. Since some of the conclusions have to do with the artist's emotions embodied in his works, Freud's statements have a bearing on the aesthetic character of Leonardo's works.

And this leads to the aesthetic pertinence of Freud's comments on Mona Lisa's smile, which he regarded as probably a highly-charged emotional symbol for Leonardo. The emotional charge on this detail—like an emotionally-charged gesture in a heated discussion—would be caught by a sensitive observer as a very significant element in the appreciation of the work of art. The observer would not necessarily know *why* it was so heavily charged with emotion but would feel *that* it was and that it was relevant to the appreciation of the work. This would explain the fascination Gautier and Pater and all the other emotionally-sensitive writers of the nineteenth century found in the smile, and the fact that the smile and the expression of the *Mona Lisa* rarely go unmentioned in any comment on the portrait even by so matter-of-fact a critic as Vasari.

Boas' point, however, is that here is another interpretation added to that of the romantics, and one to be distinguished from that of the earlier critics mainly interested in realism and technical finish.

Boas then notes that lately the interest in the *Mona Lisa* seems to have declined, partly in reaction perhaps to the emotional interpretations of it offered by the nineteenth-century romantics, but mostly because the fashionable criticism of art in the recent decades is either Marxian or nonrepresentational, and the *Mona Lisa* does not attract exceptional attention on either of these scores.

Boas terminates his recording of the four and a half centuries of commentary on the *Mona Lisa* with a sentence from Leonardo's notebooks. "Women," Leonardo says, "should be represented in modest attitudes with legs close together, arms folded, and their heads low and bending sideways." Thus Boas makes a whole circle back to the beginning. And I suppose his insinuation is that Leonardo was a plain, sensible, red-blooded fellow who looked facts in the face with no funny business and, when he was asked to paint a portrait of a merchant's wife, he painted it with proper care and accepted the proper fee. If you want the artist's intention, here it is; and all the rest, from Vasari to Pater and Freud, is froth and has nothing to do with the picture, though it is informative of the temper of the times when Vasari, Pater, Freud, and the others wrote.

And yet you remember that in the opening section of this essay Boas stated that "to define the work of art as the work intended by the artist gives us only the slenderest clues to appropriate standards for judging it."

The concluding paragraph of Boas' paper runs as follows: "Our purpose in this paper has been merely to show how a given work of art may in different periods have essentially different content—and therefore be admired for different, if not for contradictory, reasons. If this instance is typical, it would appear that works of art which 'withstand the test of time' change their natures as the times change. The work of art becomes thus the locus of a new set of values determined by the preconceptions or the predominant interest of the new critic or observer." [3]

If this conclusion is taken literally—and I don't see how else we can take it, though I also don't see how Boas can wish it to be taken so—the so-called *Mona Lisa* is a physical locus (a canvas? or a "name"?) which by chance was the locus of a succession of entirely discrete perceptual projections. From 1550 for a century or two it was a structure of meticulous representation and technical finish. Then it ceased to be both of these and around 1850 became the locus of emotional expression. Then it ceased to be any of these and around 1900 became a piece of clinical evidence and an embodiment of certain unconscious motivations.

Now, of course, the opposite thesis of this book is that the *Mona Lisa* as an object of criticism was all of these all the time. All that is needed to make this clear is a complete analysis of the work of art, from which the distinctions among the physical vehicle, the perceptions of it, and the object of criticism emerge. Particular perceptions differ with the mood of the moment, the discriminatory powers of the spectator, the cultural interests of the time, but the physical vehicle is fairly stable; and the object of criticism as the structure of relevant traits that tend to be selected and funded for the object of criticism on the stimulus of the vehicle is also quite stable. What Boas fails to take account of is the selective process generating the object of criticism, with the result that the work of art collapses under his analysis into a heap of unrelated perceptions or cultural projections.

Of course, from the moment Leonardo finished the *Mona Lisa*, the picture was nearly all the things the long line of discriminating critics discovered it was. It was a remarkable piece of realism, a skillful exemplification of artistry, a rich embodiment of emotion, and quite surely an expression of some unconscious drives. Vasari was clearly much moved by it. In spite of the emphasis of his time upon realism and technique, he could not resist remarking that while looking at the portrait "one thinks it rather divine than human." And it would be hard to believe Gautier and Pater did not recognize the artistry and realism of the *Mona Lisa* while trying to put in words the specific emotion it aroused in them through its visual forms and associations. And Freud, of course, did not ignore Pater but believed he was amplifying and deepening the understanding of the emotion Pater found embodied there. And so on from critic to critic. Not but what there were many irrelevancies, to be shed in the progress towards the determination of the object of criticism. But the trend over the centuries has been to amplify and deepen the understanding of the *Mona Lisa*, not to whittle it away and nullify it.

I wonder if Boas realizes that by his mode of analysis no man would have a determinate character of his own—not even George Boas himself—but only his name and possibly his anatomy. Even the chair upon which I sit would dissolve into a name. For suppose A describes its color, and B its texture, and C its utility, and D its artistry, and E its comfortableness. And, to complete the analogy, let these descriptions be spread out through time so that none of them occurs simultaneously with another. Does that demonstrate that there is a totally different chair for each of these spectators? When C reports on its utility, does that mean that he has no awareness of its colors, texture, artistry, and comfortableness? Even if C happens to be color-blind, does that imply that the chair is colorless? Not at all. And, similarly, neither does Boas' collection of varied reports imply that the *Mona Lisa* has not continuously possessed the various properties which the various critics have chosen to stress. The service these critics have done is to show us that for the fullest appreciation we should discriminate them all.

This, I think, is a sufficient answer to the attack on the object of criticism that lies implicit in an extreme form of relativism such as Boas seems to espouse. But the sort of answer I prefer would be a more positive one for a man of such wide and discriminating taste as George Boas possesses. It would consist in observing him carrying out his discriminations in the presence of some excellent work that he admires. Something of this sort happens several times in *Wingless Pegasus*. But I would particularly ask that one read or reread the pages where Boas is describing some of the details he finds in Milton's sonnet on his dead wife. Boas is here expressing his annoyance at a group of critics who try to shut out as relevant to a poem associations which require some knowledge that cannot be obtained entirely from within a poem, such as the knowledge of Milton's blindness. At the height of his indignation over the effects of such criticism, Boas writes: "Since most readers read the sonnet with their whole minds, they will interpret it in the light of all they know, and will not attempt to impoverish its meaning by deliberately and, I venture to say, arbitrarily lopping off *relevance* which is actually there" (italics mine).

And so with the *Mona Lisa* or any other work of art as an object of criticism, I only ask the responsible critic that he shall not attempt to impoverish its meaning by deliberately and, I venture to say, arbitrarily lopping off relevance which is actually there.

6

THE CONCEPT OF FUSION IN DEWEY'S AESTHETIC THEORY

ABOUT A THIRD of the way through *Art as Experience,* after duly deploring the frequent hypostatization of "beauty" into a hardened essence, Dewey ventures to define the term as "the response to that which to reflection is the consummated movement of matter integrated through its inner relations into a single qualitative whole." That which is primarily indicated by this definition as the aesthetic value is the "single qualitative whole," which is to be vividly had in the immediacy of the experience present. "The purpose of esthetic art," he writes further on, is "the enhancement of direct experience itself. . . ."

With this central theme of Dewey's aesthetics and his eagerness to bring it to the attention of his contemporaries we are all familiar. But attention has not been drawn so emphatically to the underlying conceptions of "fusion" and "funding" through which an experience or a situation acquires just the unique character it has. For "the single qualitative whole" acquires this singleness of quality only by way of "the consummated movement of matter through its inner relations," or, in other terms of Dewey's, through the fusion and funding of the details entering into the experience.

It could even be held that fusion and funding are the more primitive concepts for this aesthetics, since the single quality follows inevitably from the process of fusion and funding. Moreover, if one desires to make discriminations among a variety of unique aesthetic qualities, one can only do so by analyzing what has been fused and funded. Fusion is the bridge for this aesthetics between the utter uniqueness of the quality of an experience and the analysis or inquiry about it. If it were not that the quality of an experience consisted in the fusion of details which may enter into many other experiences, every quality would be insulated from every other beyond hope of intercommunication, and the intuition of quality would be so completely ineffable that no symbol could ever presumably have been suggested for it.

So I wish in this analysis to direct attention to these crucial concepts of fusion and funding. Both terms are common all through Dewey's writings. Of the two, fusion is the more general term, and funding may be regarded as fusion which involves memory or elements coming out of the past. I think I am safe in saying that Dewey would not use funding to refer to dated and articulated memory, but only when the memory elements give a tone and a trend to an experience—in short, when they fuse into its single total quality.

It is a remarkable thing how few references to fusion and funding one finds in the indexes to Dewey's chief works. He has much, of course, to say about quality, but never, so far as I have found, does he stop to write on the topic of fusion or funding. He used the concepts all the time but never held them up for long and careful scrutiny. Suppose we try to do just this thing.

To begin with, some typical passage in which he deals with quality and fusion will be convenient. Take the following: "I have previously noted that artist and perceiver alike begin with what may be called a total seizure, an inclusive qualitative whole not yet articulated, not distinguished into members . . . .

"Even at the outset, the total massive quality has its uniqueness; even when vague and undefined, it is just that which it is and not anything else. If the perception continues, discrimination inevitably sets in. Attention must move, and, as it moves, parts, members, emerge from the background. And if attention moves in a unified direction instead of wandering, it is controlled by a pervading qualitative unity; attention is controlled *by* it because it operates within it . . . Not only must this quality be in all 'parts,' but it can only be felt, that is, immediately experienced. I am not trying to describe it, for it cannot be described nor even be *specifically* pointed at—since whatever is specified in a work of art is one of *its* differentiations. . . .

"But the penetrating quality that runs through all the parts of a work of art and binds them into an individualized whole can only be emotionally 'intuited.' The different elements and specific qualities of a work of art blend and fuse in a way which physical things cannot emulate. This fusion is the felt presence of the same qualitative unity in all of them. 'Parts' are discriminated, not intuited. But without the intuited enveloping quality, parts are external to one another and mechanically related. Yet the organism which is the work of art is nothing different from its parts or members. It *is* the parts as members—a fact that again brings us to the one pervasive quality that remains the same quality in being differentiated. The resulting sense of totality is commemorative, expectant, insinuating, premonitory." [1]

A good many of the characteristics of fusion and the quality it develops are exhibited in this passage.

(1) First, it is clear that there is no actual difference between "fusion" and the single quality that results from it. The process of fusion is not one thing occurring at one time and the resulting single quality another thing at a later time. The process of fusion *is*, in the very process itself, the quality fused: "The different elements and specific qualities of a work of art blend and fuse. . . . The fusion is the felt presence of the same qualitative unity in all of them."

(2) The elements fused have all sorts of references—to the present, the past, the future, and the unconscious—"commemorative, expectant, insinuating." The elements fused are not only those immediately present in the focus of conscious attention but those that come from any area of the "fringe," and even from sources out-

side of what can be brought to conscious attention.[2]

(3) The elements fused are themselves qualitative.

(4) The quality of the fusion is an object of immediacy. "It (quality) can only be felt." Dewey adds that fused quality cannot "be described nor . . . *specifically* pointed out," which is in one sense ridiculous, since, clearly, he is quite successfully indicating it and doing well at giving some sort of description of it. Many philosophers when they approach one of their ultimate categorial elements delight in casting the halo of ineffability about it. The unspeakability of the element, however, must be of a specially defined sort, since by some other sense of utterability they are presenting it for belief by means of speech. All Dewey evidently means by indescribability in this passage is the character of ultimate immediacy. And he suggests that "intuition" be stipulated to symbolize this sort of apprehension of immediacy.

(5) Qualitative fusion is a process which always has some duration and may spread over an extended period. In aesthetic experience it is likely to begin in "a seizure . . . not yet ar-

ticulated." But "if perception continues, discrimination inevitably sets in." Though the unity of the quality remains, the elements fused become clearer and "emerge from the background." Elsewhere the process of fusion is shown by Dewey to reside in a purposive act, as in the artist's act of creation and a spectator's act of critical appreciation. It follows that the qualitative unity of the purposive act allows not only for degrees of articulation of the elements fused but for redistributions of these with different emphases on the focus. Moreover, an original seizure may be regarded later as in a way an error. "The outcome of discrimination will often be to convince us that the particular thing in question was not worthy of calling out the rapt seizure; that in fact the latter was caused by factors adventitious to the object itself." The singleness of quality intuited thus allows for certain changes of quality within its unity—such as degrees of articulation of the elements fused, various distributions of focus and fringe, even admission of error regarding relations of elements to an object referred to. In problematic purposive activity, for instance, it is the single quality that guides the process, correcting the errors (which do enter into the process, to be sure) and confirming the successes.

(6) It is the quality through the process of fusion that controls and determines the unity of a work of art, of an artist's creative activity, indeed of any purposive activity, and ultimately and categorially the extent and boundaries of what Dewey calls a "situation." The passage quoted confirms the first statements, but the last are best exemplified in an important article to which he twice refers in *Art as Experience* entitled "Qualitative Thought." * Fusion thus acquires a cosmic significance for Dewey, being the crucial agency for distinguishing one event from another.

Some of these characters of fusion appear to be inconsistent with others. Let us name the characters simply. (1) Fusion *is* quality, (2) fusion (quality) has references or meaning, (3) what is fused is itself qualitative (and so fused?), (4) fusion is a single felt immediacy, (5) fusion (quality) is a process, may change, may be in error, (6) fusion controls an event, situation, process, and defines its boundaries.

* This essay is included in the collection of essays entitled *Philosophy and Civilization*, Putnam's, 1931.

(1) appears self-contradictory, (4) appears contrary to (2) and (5), (3) seems to involve an infinite regression. Yet all of these characters can be found in the passage quoted. Granted that Dewey often writes impressionistically, and that the emergence of a new concept can perhaps only be indicated in some such way, the question is legitimate as to whether the concept is fact or fiction. If fact, the stressing of the concept is one of Dewey's most notable contributions. But if fact, it is still not very clearly defined or indicated.

Before going further, let us ask how new is this conception? For if it were limited to Dewey, this might be strong ground for questioning its factuality. But nearly all pragmatists of note do stress it in some degree—notably William James and Bergson. Croce's intuition is probably based on the same insight. Its first appearance in aesthetics, however, is possibly Baumgarten's definition of aesthetic experience as clear but *confused* cognition. For the connotation of "confused" as the opposite of "distinct" is for Baumgarten very close to Dewey's "fused." So the idea of fused quality has a respectable history.

Can some clarification be given which will

remove the hovering contradictions in Dewey's depiction of fusion? One possibility is that fusion is not a single concept but a cluster of concepts. Could a list of illustrations of fusions help? Let me try:

(A) Fusion of sensations in immediate presentation such as the quality of a chord in music (fusion of C, E, G for quality of tonic triad) or of William James's lemonade (fusion of sensory qualities of lemon, sugar, and water).

(B) Fusion of "fringe" with qualities in the focus of attention, such as the effect of context of sensory stimuli on a sensation in the center of interest—the character of an oblique line depending on its placement in a rectangle, for instance.

(C) Fusion of before and after in the shifting focus of a "specious present." For instance, the fusions of past and coming pitches and rhythms in the hearing of a melody.

(D) Fusion of memories with present sensations (funding).

(E) Fusion of an extended scheme or form with the materials in the focus of attention which serves to unfold it. James writes, "How comes it about that a man reading something aloud for the first time is able immediately to emphasize all his words aright, unless from the very first he have a sense of at least the form of the sentence yet to come, which sense is fused with his consciousness of the present word, and modifies its emphasis in his mind so as to make him give it the proper accent as he utters it"? [3] It is the same with the form of a purposive act, compositional forms in art, etc.

(F) Fusion for recognition, as in the instantaneous recognition of a word or a face where it would be difficult to say what we recognize the object by. It is the same with an artist's style.

(G) Fusion for intuitive induction (hunches).

(H) Fusion for emotional quality under emotional stress, as in fright, rage, etc.

(I) Fusion in the absorbed perception of an aesthetic object.

(J) Fusion of elements of a problem for guidance towards a purposive solution.

Are these all the same thing? Or are some reducible to others? Are there still other forms of fusion?

The simplest of these instances to deal with is the first, for here the situation is transparent. The elements fused are all present and easily controllable, and the fusion of them can be made or unmade, in many instances, at will. A person with a fairly discriminating ear can listen to a tonic triad as a single quality or as a combination of three distinguishable pitches simultaneously presented. He can listen to the three notes as fused or unfused or fused again. If he needs a little help, the notes may be played singly so that he senses clearly the specific quality of each. Then they can be simultaneously combined, and he can discriminate them in combination, and then he can relax (in some sense) and let the fused quality of the total chord register. The fused quality seems to be the easier, more "natural" way of listening to the combination of its notes. To discriminate the specific pitches fused takes an effort of attention or else training in discrimination so that one is familiar with the analysis to be expected.

Moreover, the quality of a sensory fusion alters with the relative intensities of the qualities fused. A musical timbre was something of a mystery until experimental analysis showed that it consisted of nothing else but simultaneous combinations of pitches at various intensities but highly *fused*. A very discriminating ear can analyze many timbres with considerable accuracy. But here the fusion is persistent and the analysis very difficult. Fusion seems to be the natural, easy, primitive mode of perception, and analysis the difficult mode requiring effort or training. That suggests that analyzed perception develops only under practical stress for the solution of conflicts in problematic situations. Analysis is the product of practical and cognitive perception. Fusion is the normal state of consummatory perception. The organism is thus biased in favor of fusion and is driven to analysis only by the struggle for life and the avoidance of frustration. Then we may notice that, in man, sight, on which he depends for most of his practical discrimination, presents most easily the most analytically discriminating perceptions, and touch the next. Hearing tends much more strongly to fusion, and taste and smell still more so, savors being very hard to analyze by most men. As for our internal sensations, these seem to be almost incapable of discriminating analysis.

Fusion then seems to be the state of consciousness to be found *unless* a problematic situation arises forcing discrimination and analysis to avoid pain and frustration. Fusion, accordingly, is not a process added to primitive elements generating a new supervening quality.

Rather, analysis is the added process breaking into a primitive fusion generating a discrimination of some of the elements lying in the fusion. The continuity of life is a gradation of qualitative fusions, here and there broken into by articulated analyses and discriminations wherever practical exigencies require it.

If this is the clue (and it complies with James's stream of consciousness as well as Dewey's contexts of experience) we begin to see our own way through the other illustrations of fusion and to find a solution for some of the apparent contradictions.

First, it is not a self-contradiction that a quality is a fusion. The quality is what is immediately intuited as it is. At the same time the content of the quality is complex and related to many other things. The complexity and relatedness are registered in the quality and are what (on analysis) make it just the quality it is and not some other. When the quality is analyzed and discriminations made within it, then the connection of the discriminated elements with the quality as unanalyzed can be clearly traced. (The separate notes can be traced into the single unique character of the chord.) There would be a self-contradiction only if the experience of the single quality were at the same time the experience of discriminated elements. But a discrimination of the elements of a quality is *not* the intuition of the quality itself. All that fusion denotes is the special connection between these two experiences, together with the observation that the elements discriminated do not utterly vanish from existence when they return to the state of an intuited quality, since the quality intuited is observed to consist of the mutual qualification of the earlier discriminated qualities.

The one correction of any great significance that seems to be needed in Dewey's general treatment of quality and fusion has to do with his emphasis on the singleness of quality. Actually the intuited quality will change with every change in the elements fused. But if the change is, proportionately to the other elements present, not great, we continue to speak of it as the same quality. We speak of the quality of lemonade remaining the same even though an increase in the quantity of sugar changes its quality. We say it is a sweeter or a more sour lemonade. Literally each change of sweetness is a change of intuited quality. In one passage Dewey acknowledges this fact in a startling phrase: "A new poem is created by every one who reads

poetically." When he insists so frequently that
a work of art is bound together by its quality
and this is what guides the artist, and the perceiver, and also the critic in seeking his judgment of it, a reader might well wonder what he
could mean by the quoted statement. But, of
course, strictly speaking, not only every reader
but every reading creates a new quality. In fact,
a new quality (and, therefore, and, in a certain
precise sense, a new poem) is created in every
specious present through the period of the one
reader's reading. But what holds these different
qualities (taken in this very precise sense) together is their qualitative similarity which *on
analysis* turns out to consist of the constancy of
the organization of elements fused. The fusion
is always of elements in the organization, however changing the distribution and relative intensities of the elements in every specific fusion.

As one reads the poem, the focus of attention
is on the details of the specious present. But
these details in the focus are related in their
aesthetic organization to the details already read
and to those yet to come. The details already
read are funded into the present focus of attention, and expectancies are aroused for details
yet to come. As the focus of attention slides

across the total organization of the poem, the specific fusion differs in quality at each moment. But part of the quality of the fusion at each moment is in the quality of the total pattern of the poem gradually being revealed and progressively thickening in expectancy until finally confirmed at the conclusion of the reading. On a later reading the total quality of the pattern is completely present at every stage of the reading, but the specific quality of the moment constantly changes with a redistribution of the relative vividness of details.

In sum, the singleness of quality Dewey emphasizes so much is the quality of the total pattern, which fuses into the indefinite variety of specific qualities of immediate perceptual appreciation. Again, there is no inconsistency if the process of fusion is faithfully described exactly as it occurs. Both statements turn out to be true: that a well-made work of art is controlled by a single quality, and that every perception of a work of art is different in quality from every other.

The solution of the paradox becomes clear, however, only after the discriminating analysis of the elements that were fused in the qualities referred to. There appears on analysis to be a

determinate set of details organized in a determinate pattern. The totality of these details as
integrally related in the pattern is funded into
every aesthetically attentive perception of the
work. This phase of the qualitative intuition of
the work remains constant and is a single controlling quality for the relevancy of details in
the work. At the same time each specific intuition of the work has a different focus and fringe
which generates a different specific quality for
every intuitive perception. But all of these specific qualities are controlled and accounted for
by the controlling quality.

Referring this distinction back to our analysis
of the work of art in Chapter One, we see that the
specific quality is the fusion occurring in any
single perception stimulated by the vehicle,
whereas the *controlling quality* is the fusion of
the relevant details in the object of criticism.

This distinction between controlling quality
and specific intuited quality will, I believe, take
care of most of the remaining inconsistencies
hovering in Dewey's exposition.

The concept of singleness of quality is ambiguous. It can mean either the singleness of
the controlling quality or that of the specific
intuited quality of a moment of immediacy. The

singleness of the controlling quality is consistent with a multiplicity of specific intuited qualities. So, in respect to the controlling quality, the
intuited quality may change, may even be in
error. And in respect to the intuited quality, the
controlling quality has the function of determining what is or is not relevant to a situation
or a purpose or a problem.

As for the list of illustrations of fusion, and
the question as to whether there are one or several kinds, the distinction between a controlling
and a specific quality would appear to me to
supply an adequate answer. In some of these
illustrations one is dominant and in some the
other, and in some there is a balance. These differences of emphasis seem adequate to account
for the different characters of fusion in the
series of examples. For instance, in emotional
fusion the specific quality is stressed; in the
hunches of intuitive induction, the controlling
quality is stressed; in the appreciative perception of an aesthetic object, the two are balanced.

What about the threat of an infinite regress,
if every quality is a fusion? The fusion of a fusion, of course, provides no problem and can
easily be confirmed by inspection. There is no
question but that an instrumental timbre is a

fusion, nor that a tonic chord on a piano is a fusion of three tones with piano timbre. Better still, an orchestral effect is ordinarily a fusion of different instrumental timbres. Every fusion is a fusion of qualities and the qualities fused are often demonstrably fusions. The interesting question is whether there are simple elemental qualities that are not fusions. This is a very interesting question, in fact, and has far-reaching implications. The immediate intuition of un-analyzable elementary sense qualities like sweet, salt, a determinate color, or a determinate pitch, are not decisive. To immediate intuition many timbres and odors appear elementary and simple which by indirect evidence can be shown to be complex fusions. It is possible that the elementary sense qualities of our "discriminanda schemes" (as Tolman calls them) are themselves fusions of qualities for which we lack the psychological and physiological mechanisms for discrimination. But, by extrapolation, it could still be argued that there must be subliminal elemental qualities to fuse into the qualities of the sensations we intuit as elementary. There is, however, another possible hypothesis. That is that atomic qualitative elements are never reached but that qualities are intrinsically fusions of field structures which interpenetrate; and that, in fact, a fusion is precisely a qualitative record of a cosmic field, which may receive a quantitative analytical description in terms of physical and physiological units. This sort of idea is consonant with the thinking of Dewey too, for whom the "knowledge" of an event and the "having" of it are complementary aspects. Still more characteristic of him is the insistence that the qualitative or the aesthetic is not detached from life or physical events, but that the two are intimately entangled with each other, and that each is revelatory of the other. So, I am here suggesting that his fertile concept of fusion is coextensive with that of quality and enters into every event that quality does.

Dewey concludes his essay on "Qualitative Thought" with a paragraph that contains these words: "I have touched, as I am well aware, only upon the fringes of a complex subject. But in view of the general neglect of the subject, I shall be satisfied if I have turned the attention of those interested in thought and its workings to an overlooked field. . . . the gist of the matter is that the immediate existence of quality, and of dominant and pervasive quality, is the background, the point of departure, and the regulative principle of all thinking." [4]

We are still "on the fringes" of the subject, but Dewey has indicated the "dominant and pervasive quality" of the problem, and it only remains for us to follow his lead.

NOTES

CHAPTER ONE

1. George Santayana, *The Sense of Beauty* (New York: Charles Scribner's Sons, 1896), p. 193, pp. 194-5, p. 197. Used by permission of the publishers.

2. Bernard Bosanquet, *Three Lectures on Aesthetic* (London: Macmillan and Co., Ltd., 1923), pp. 47-49.

CHAPTER THREE

1. For an extended treatment of these theories together with the interest or satisfaction theory associated with the mechanistic philosophy, see the author's *The Basis of Criticism in the Arts* (Cambridge: Harvard Univ. Press, 1949).

2. Andrew Ushenko, *Dynamics of Art* (Bloomington: Indiana Univ. Press, 1953), p. 31, p. 52.

CHAPTER FIVE

1. George Boas, *Wingless Pegasus* (Baltimore: The Johns Hopkins Press, 1950), p. 211, p. 33, p. 31. By courtesy of the Johns Hopkins Press.

2. *Ibid.*, p. 213 ff.

3. *Ibid.*, p. 235.

CHAPTER SIX

Reproduced by permission of *The Journal of Aesthetics and Art Criticism,* Vol. XII, No. 2, December, 1953, pp. 169-76.

1. John Dewey, *Art as Experience* (New York: Minton, Balch & Co., 1934), pp. 191-3. By permission of G. P. Putnam's Sons.

2. Cf. *Art as Experience,* p. 72, for a reference to materials on the unconscious.

3. William James, *Principles of Psychology,* Vol. I (New York: Henry Holt & Co., 1890), pp. 253-4. Quoted by permission of the publishers.

4. John Dewey, *Philosophy and Civilization* (New York: Minton, Balch & Co., 1931), p. 116. By permission of G. P. Putnam's Sons.